AN INTRODUCTION TO DATA ANALYSIS USING MINITAB® FOR WINDOWS

THIRD EDITION

Dorothy Wakefield
Kathleen McLaughlin

PEARSON
Prentice Hall

Upper Saddle River, NJ 07458

Editor-in-Chief: Sally Yagan
Executive Acquisitions Editor: Petra Recter
Supplement Editor: Joanne Wendelken
Media Project Manager: Jacquelyn Riotto Zupic
Vice President of Production & Manufacturing: David W. Riccardi
Executive Managing Editor: Kathleen Schiaparelli
Managing Editor: Nicole Jackson
Production Editor: Donna Crilly
Supplement Cover Management: Paul Gourhan
Supplement Cover Designer: Christopher Kossa
Manufacturing Manager: Trudy Pisciotti
Manufacturing Buyer: Ilene Kahn

© 2005 Pearson Education, Inc.
Pearson Prentice Hall
Pearson Education, Inc.
Upper Saddle River, NJ 07458

Printed in the United States of America

10 9 8 7 6 5 4

ISBN 0-13-149783-9

Pearson Education Ltd., *London*
Pearson Education Australia Pty. Ltd., *Sydney*
Pearson Education Singapore, Pte. Ltd.
Pearson Education North Asia Ltd., *Hong Kong*
Pearson Education Canada, Inc., *Toronto*
Pearson Educación de Mexico, S.A. de C.V.
Pearson Education—Japan, *Tokyo*
Pearson Education Malaysia, Pte. Ltd.

This book is dedicated to our families:
Fred, Madison, Anna, Hayley, Ryan, Hannah, Jack, Rob, Dan, and Chrissy who are "significantly" wonderful. (P=.00000)

Introduction

....

This MINITAB lab manual is designed to be used with any Elementary Statistics textbook. The lessons are self-explanatory and explore topics that are covered in all elementary texts.

Each chapter has an instructional section which summarizes a basic statistical concept. This is followed by a computer assignment in which students can practice the techniques that they have learned in the chapter.

All the data sets used in the lessons are saved on the included data CD as MINITAB Worksheets (*.MTW).

All instructions and diagrams in the manual were developed using MINITAB Release 14. Users of the Student Version of MINITAB may find some slight differences in the procedures.

Our purpose in writing this manual is to provide some simple examples of basic statistical techniques so that students can see that statistics is more than just a long list of mind-boggling formulas. Since MINITAB does all the computation, students can concentrate on selecting the appropriate statistical method and can focus on understanding and interpreting the results.

Note to Instructors:

All MINITAB worksheets used in the Assignment sections have multiple versions numbered from 1 to 6. For example, in Problem 1 of Assignment 1 the file ETHNIC1.MTW is used. ETHNIC2.MTW through ETHNIC6.MTW also exist on the Data CD. Our intention was to provide different data so that an instructor can vary the assignments from semester to semester.

Table of Contents

Students will run hypothesis tests to compare two means for two independent samples, two dependent samples, and for two non-normal samples.

Students will study two-variables datasets, construct scatterplots, and run correlation and regression analyses.

Chapter 1

Qualitative Data Analysis

QUALITATIVE DATA is another name for categorical data. That is, the data is count data indicating the number of observations that fall into each category. For example, the chairperson of the Math Department might be interested in the number of males and females taking a Calculus course. In this example, the categories are Male and Female, and we would simply count how many students are in each category.

Once the data has been collected, it is necessary to summarize the data so that it is easier to understand the overall pattern. The data can be presented in a frequency table, but more often it is displayed graphically using either a bar chart or a pie chart. In general, a graphical display is both simple to make and easy to understand. The goal is to give the reader a quick overview of the data with just a look at the picture. Many newspapers and magazines use these graphs to get a reader's attention. We will be learning how to create bar charts and pie charts using MINITAB.

Bar Charts

Bar charts are very simple to create using MINITAB. One thing to keep in mind is that any chart is incomplete without proper labeling. A title should describe the data in a short phrase. The graph should also have labels on both the x-axis and the y-axis. Normally the x-axis will have the different categories, so the axis label should describe the categories. The y-axis will have the counts or frequency for each category, so the axis label may be as simple as 'frequency' or 'count'.

For this practice example we will open a MINITAB worksheet named **ENROLL.MTW** which contains data that shows the percentage of students by School/College who actually enrolled at the University after being admitted for the years 2001–2003.

To do this, click on: FILE → OPEN WORKSHEET.

On the screen that appears, you must tell MINITAB that the worksheet is on your CD-ROM. Your CD drive is usually your **d: drive**. To select the CD drive, click on the down arrow beside the **Look in** field and click on **Compact Disc (D:)**. (Fig. 1-1)

• •
Fig. 1-1

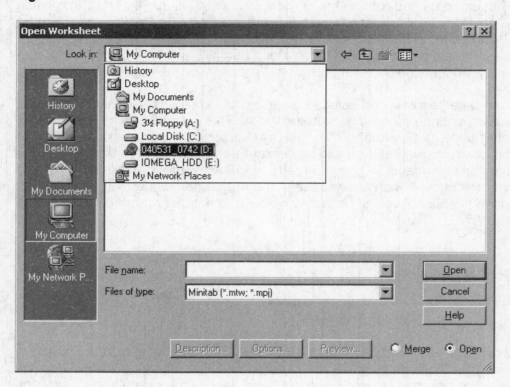

A list of all the datasets on the CD should appear on the screen. To open the worksheet **ENROLL**, click on **ENROLL** and then click on **Open**. (Fig. 1-2)

• •
Fig. 1-2

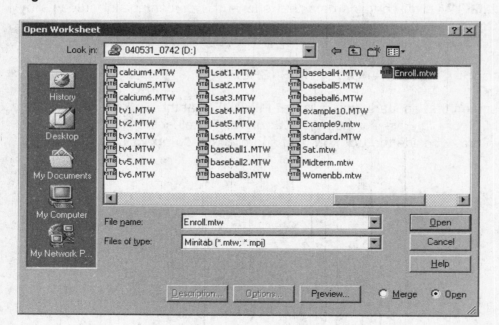

The spreadsheet in the Data Window should now contain the data that we want to use. Notice that the data is from 3 different years: 2001, 2002, and 2003. To begin, we will use only the data from 2001 to create a bar chart. Column 3 (C3), called YIELD, contains the percentage of accepted students who actually enrolled for each school in 2001 and C2, called SCHOOL, contains the categories. In this case, the categories are the names of the different schools within a university. The YEAR in which the data was collected is in C1.

To create the bar chart, click on: GRAPH → BAR CHART

The following pop-up screen will appear. Click on the down arrow beside the field **Bars represent** and select **Values from a table.** Highlight a **Simple** bar chart and click **OK**. (Fig. 1-3)

●●●●●●●●●●●●●●●●●●●●●●
Fig. 1-3

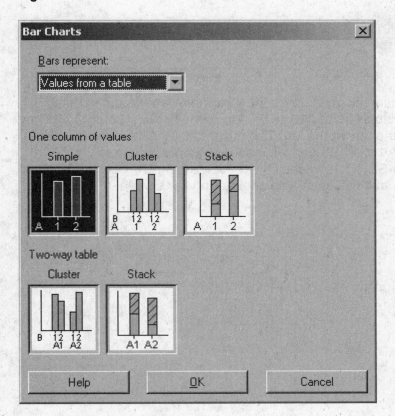

The main bar chart input screen (Fig. 1-4) has many options that you can select. You can select the options before drawing the chart, or once the chart is drawn, you can edit the chart to make any desired changes.

• •

Fig. 1-4

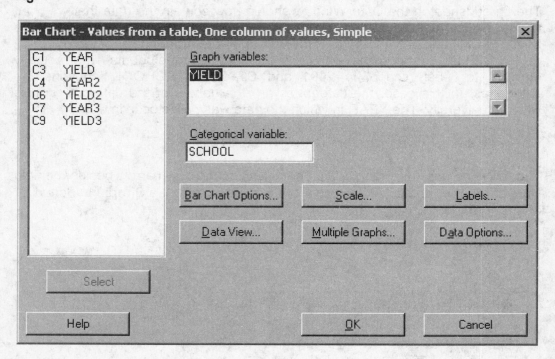

Minitab is expecting a numeric variable for the **Graph variables** and will only
display the numeric variables in the box to the left of the screen. Select YIELD by
double-clicking on it in the box at the left. Tab down to the field labeled
Categorical variable. A list of categorical variables should appear in the box at
the left. Double-click on SCHOOL to select it. If you click on **OK** now, a bar chart
using all of Minitab's default values should appear on your screen. (Fig. 1-5)

• •

Fig. 1-5

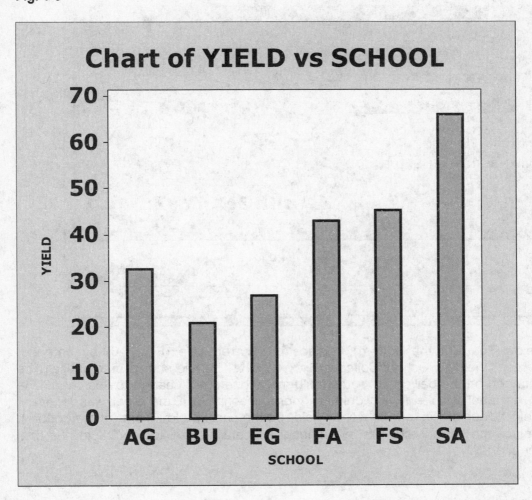

Before printing this chart, there are a few changes that will improve the
appearance and readability of the chart. You could close this graph and go back
to the GRAPH menu and enter a title, however, it is very easy to edit the chart
itself. Double-click on the title of the graph. The following screen will pop up.
(Fig. 1-6)

• •

Fig. 1-6

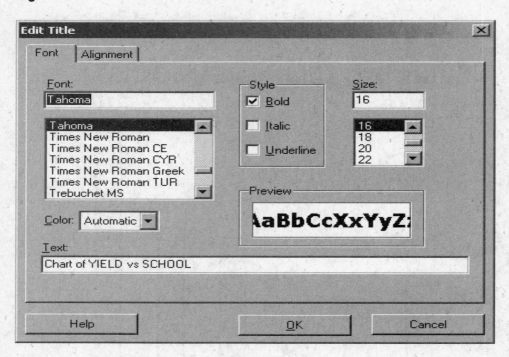

Below **Text** (at the bottom), replace the current title (Fig. 1-6) by entering: Percent Yield By School/College. Click on **OK**. The title should automatically be changed on the bar chart. You should make one other change to this chart. The y-axis label is "Yield". It would be more descriptive if the label was "Percent Yield". Double-click on the word "Yield" on the chart. Below **Text** (at the bottom), replace the current axis title by entering: Percent Yield. Click on **OK** for the final bar chart. (Fig. 1-7)

• • • • • • • • • • • • • • • • • • • •
Fig. 1-7

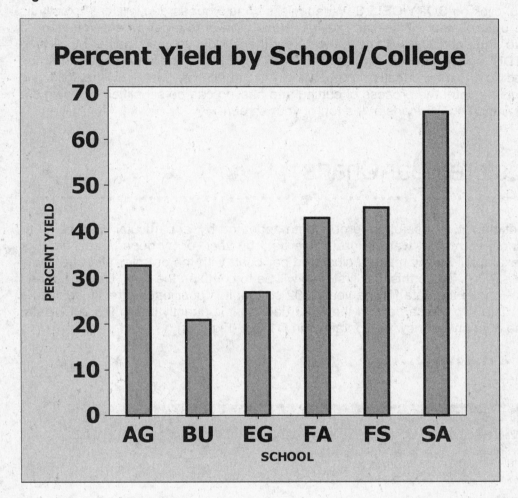

If the bar chart looks good, then you will want to print it. While the chart is still on your screen, click on: **FILE → PRINT GRAPH.** This will print the Graph Window for you. After printing the bar chart, you can close the Graph Window by clicking on the **"X"** in the upper right corner of the Graph Window. This will bring you back to the Data and Session Windows.

Cut and Paste
• •

At times, it is necessary to either combine data or separate a small subset of the data. Many Windows applications use the same method, so you may already be familiar with it. It is called CUT & PASTE. Simply make a copy of the desired block of data, and then just "paste" it into the area of the spreadsheet where you want it. To select the area of data you want to move, you must highlight it. To highlight it, position the cursor in the top left corner of the block of data. **Press and hold down** the mouse button as you move the cursor toward the lower right corner of the block of data. This method is known as "click & drag". When the entire area is highlighted, click on **EDIT** on the top menu, and from the pop-down menu, click on **COPY CELLS**. When this is done, your screen will look exactly as it did before. You will see no change. Next, click on the cell where you want to "paste" the data. This will move the cursor there. Now you can "paste" by clicking on **EDIT** again, but this time select **PASTE CELLS**. The data should now be added to the new location. You will be using "cut & paste" in the following example. (Note: the process of cutting and pasting can be simplified by using the COPY and PASTE icons at the top of your screen.)

Clustered Bar Charts

Sometimes it is useful to group data together by a particular variable. For instance, you might want to group the data by year, or by department, etc. For this example, we will make a clustered bar chart with the data for all three years (2001–2003). To do this, the first step will be to combine the data. Using "cut and paste", move the data for the year 2002 so that it is positioned directly below the 2001 data. Do the same with the 2003 data so it is directly below the 2002 data. All the data should now be contained in C1-C3. (Fig. 1-8)

Fig. 1-8

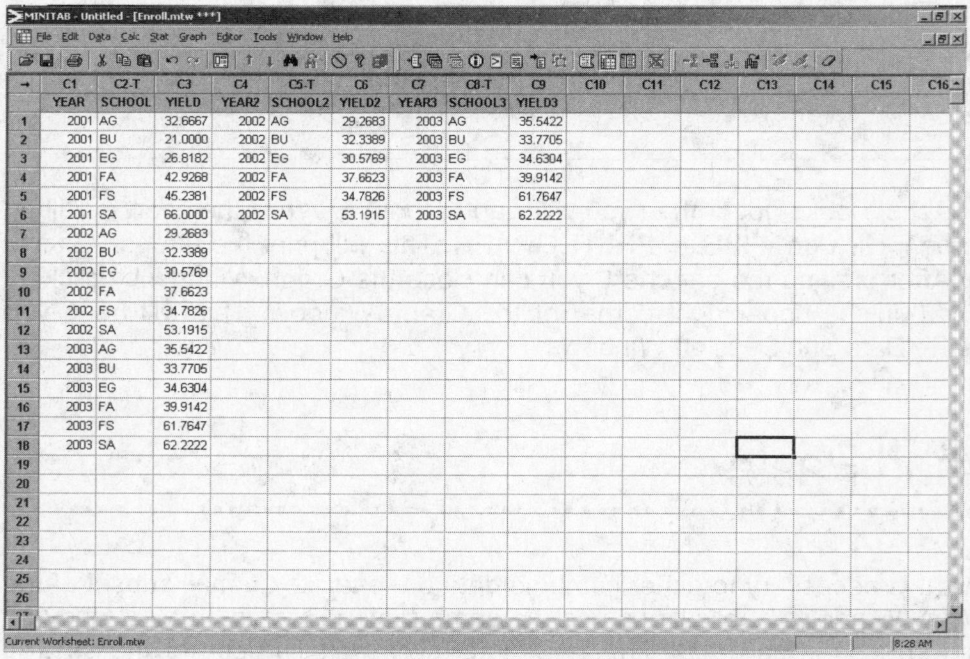

→	C1	C2-T	C3	C4	C5-T	C6	C7	C8-T	C9
	YEAR	SCHOOL	YIELD	YEAR2	SCHOOL2	YIELD2	YEAR3	SCHOOL3	YIELD3
1	2001	AG	32.6667	2002	AG	29.2683	2003	AG	35.5422
2	2001	BU	21.0000	2002	BU	32.3389	2003	BU	33.7705
3	2001	EG	26.8182	2002	EG	30.5769	2003	EG	34.6304
4	2001	FA	42.9268	2002	FA	37.6623	2003	FA	39.9142
5	2001	FS	45.2381	2002	FS	34.7826	2003	FS	61.7647
6	2001	SA	66.0000	2002	SA	53.1915	2003	SA	62.2222
7	2002	AG	29.2683						
8	2002	BU	32.3389						
9	2002	EG	30.5769						
10	2002	FA	37.6623						
11	2002	FS	34.7826						
12	2002	SA	53.1915						
13	2003	AG	35.5422						
14	2003	BU	33.7705						
15	2003	EG	34.6304						
16	2003	FA	39.9142						
17	2003	FS	61.7647						
18	2003	SA	62.2222						

MINITAB can easily do a clustered bar chart for this combined data. From the bar chart pop-up screen (GRAPH → BAR CHART), select **Values from a table** and **Cluster.** (Fig. 1-9) Click on **OK**.

Fig. 1-9

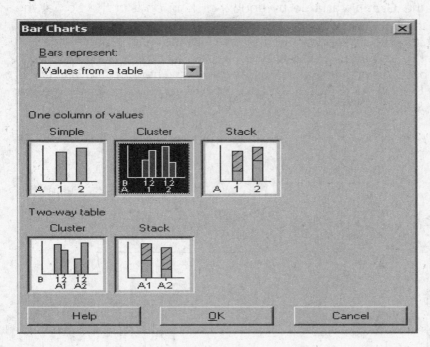

The following input screen will appear. It looks very much like the input screen used for a simple bar chart. (Fig. 1-10)

Fig. 1-10

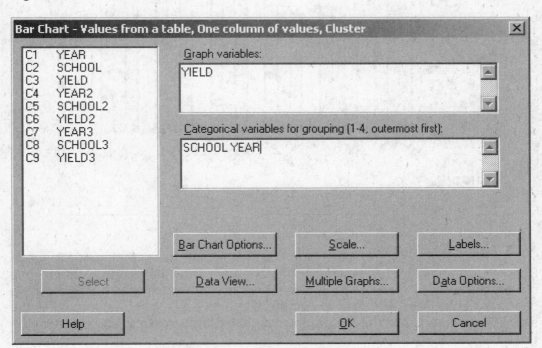

Notice that on this screen, you can enter more than one **Categorical variable**. Select YIELD for the **Graph variable** by double-clicking on it in the box at the left. Tab down to the field labeled **Categorical variables for grouping.** A list of categorical variables should appear in the box at the left. Double-click on SCHOOL to select it, and then double-click on YEAR. For each School/College, we would like a bar showing the yield for each year. Therefore, SCHOOL is selected first and then YEAR. (Fig. 1-10) Click on **OK** to view the clustered bar chart. (Fig. 1-11).

• •

Fig. 1-11

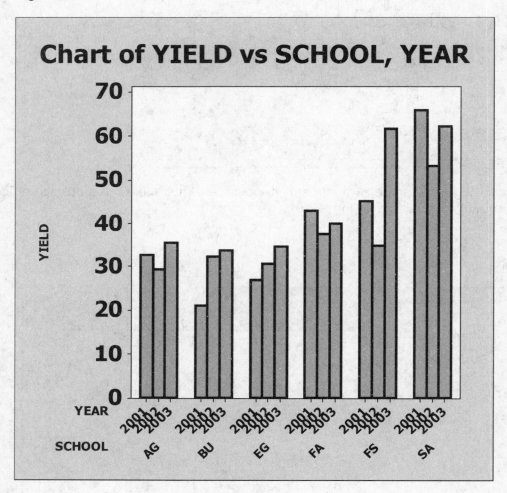

Because it is grouped, you can now see how the yield in each School/College within the university has changed over the years. Comparisons are much easier to make using a clustered bar chart rather than using separate charts for each year. Be sure to edit the title and y-axis label as you did in the simple bar chart. Now print the graph, close the Graph Window and return to the Data and Session Windows.

Pie Charts

● ●

Another way to display qualitative data is with a pie chart. Although it is harder for the eye to compare two "slices" of the pie chart than it is to compare the heights of two rectangles on a bar chart, pie charts are still very popular, especially in magazines and newspapers. Pie charts are very simple to make in MINITAB.

To create a pie chart, click on: GRAPH → PIE CHART

In the screen that appears, select **Chart values from a table** by clicking on the small circle to the left of it. The circle will be filled in with a black dot to show that you have selected it. Fill in the correct columns to identify where the data is located. For example, if you want to make a pie chart of the 2002 enrollment data, C5 (SCHOOL2) has the categories and C6 (YIELD2) has the enrollment percentages 2002. Fill in the screen as follows: **Categorical variable**: SCHOOL2 and **Summary variables**: YIELD2. (Fig. 1-12)

● ●

Fig. 1-12

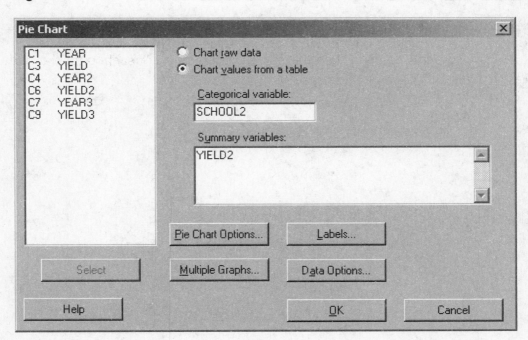

Click on **Labels** and enter an appropriate title. (Fig. 1-13)

• •

Fig. 1-13

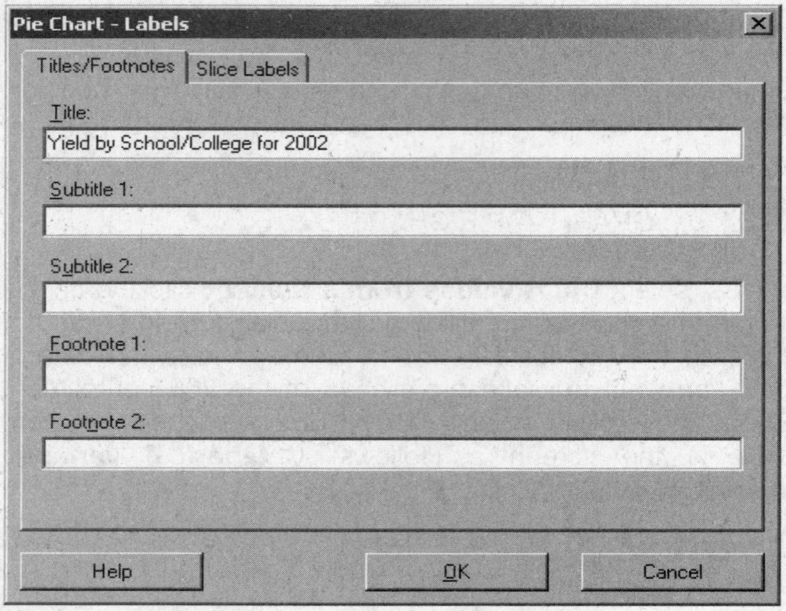

Click on the **Slice Labels** tab, and select **Frequency** and **Draw a line from label to slice** by clicking on the check boxes. Click on **OK** to view the pie chart. (Fig. 1-14) To print the chart, use the same procedure as described for the bar charts.

. . . .

Fig. 1-14

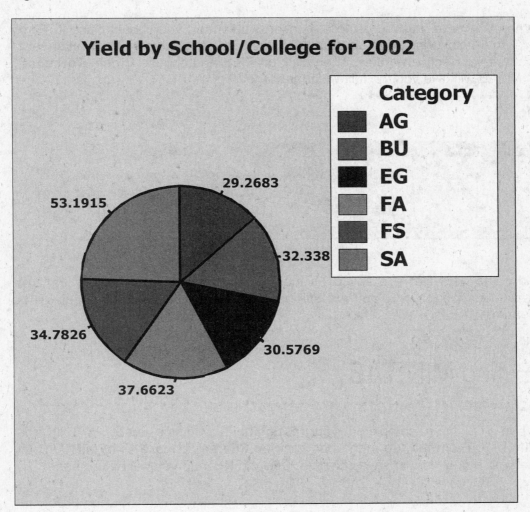

Closing a Worksheet

• •

When you have finished using a dataset (worksheet) you should close it. To do this, the Data Window must be active. Just click anywhere in the worksheet to make it your active window. Then click on **FILE** and choose **Close Worksheet**. MINITAB will give you the following message (Fig. 1-15).

• •
Fig. 1-15

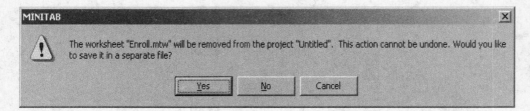

Since the data files are saved on the CD, you do **not** need to save the data again. So click on **No**. You will still be in MINITAB, but the worksheet will be cleared.

Exiting MINITAB

• •

When you have completed your assignment, you are ready to Exit from MINITAB. From the top menu bar, click on **File** and choose **Exit**. MINITAB will then ask if you want to save changes. Click on **No**, and you will be finished.

Compare the overall trend for the School of Education to the other four Schools.

3. For this example you will use the file FACULTY1.MTW. The data contained in this file is the number of faculty by school for the years 1960, 1970, 1980,1990, and 2000.

    a. Do a clustered bar chart for the data set clustering by year.

        In 1960, which school had the most faculty members? _____

        Did any school show a continuous increase in faculty throughout the period? If so, which school? _____

        Which school added the most faculty members between 1960 and 1970? _____

        Estimate the total number of faculty at this university in 1990. _____

        Which school had the greatest difference between their peak and lowest number of faculty? _____

Chapter 2

Quantitative Data Analysis

MUCH OF THE DATA that we collect is numerical, or quantitative data. Simply looking at a list of data points without organizing it in some way will not give us much information. So, particularly if the data set is large, we need techniques that we can use to summarize the data in order to get a better understanding of the data set. There are a variety of graphical techniques that are available that give excellent pictures of data sets. There are also some basic measurements of central tendency and of variation that are useful statistics to use when we are summarizing a data set. (We will study these measurements in the next chapter.) Let's begin by looking at some of the graphical techniques.

Histograms

A histogram is very similar to the bar chart that you studied in the previous lesson. The main difference is that in a histogram the data is grouped into numerical categories instead of non-numerical categories. A histogram gives you a snapshot of the data set. From this snapshot you can begin to study the distribution of the data set. Does the data appear to be symmetric or does it appear to be skewed to the left or to the right? Does the data appear to be mound-shaped (normally distributed) or does it look bimodal? When working with very small datasets, these questions about the shape of a data set can be difficult to answer. So, let's begin with two fairly large data sets, each with 100 observations.

To do this, click on: FILE → OPEN WORKSHEET

On the screen that appears, you must tell MINITAB that the worksheet is on your data CD. To do this, beside **Filename** type in **d:SAT.MTW.** The spreadsheet in the data window should now contain the Math and Verbal SAT scores in columns C1 and C2 for students accepted into the engineering program at a local university. Let's begin to analyze this data set by constructing histograms for each set of scores.

To do this, click on GRAPH → HISTOGRAM

On the pop-up screen that appears, double-click on a **Simple** histogram icon in the upper left corner of the pop-up screen. This should bring you to the main histogram screen. (Fig. 2-1)

• •
Fig. 2-1

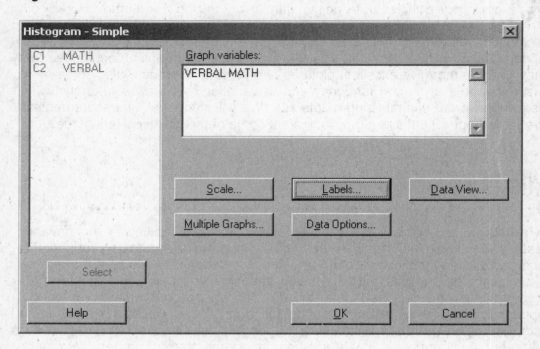

Suppose we are interested in comparing the two histograms. First select both Math and Verbal scores for the **Graph Variables** by double-clicking on them in the rectangle at the left of the pop-up. We can do this comparison most easily if the histograms are drawn using the same X and Y scales. To do this, click on the button labeled **Multiple Graphs.** On the screen that appears, choose **On separate graphs** by clicking on the circle for that choice. Then choose **Same Y** and **Same X, including same bins** by clicking on the boxes for these choices. Click on **OK**.

The next step is to put a title on the histograms. Click on the **Labels** button. This **title** will appear on both histograms. For example, you might choose the title: **SAT SCORES**. For the **Footnote**, enter your name and section number. Click on **OK.** This closes the pop-up and returns to the main histogram page. Then click on **OK** and the histograms will be produced. (Fig. 2-2). Make sure that the title, your name and section number appear on the graphs. Also, make sure the histograms have the same X and Y scales. If you are satisfied with the way the histograms look you can print the histograms. First print the active graph (the one with the blue bar across the top), clicking on **File** and selecting **Print Graph**. Close this histogram by clicking on the small **X** in the upper right corner of the graph and click **No** on the pop-up that appears. The other histogram will automatically appear. Print this histogram and then close it. (Your Data Window will now appear.)

● ●

Fig. 2-2

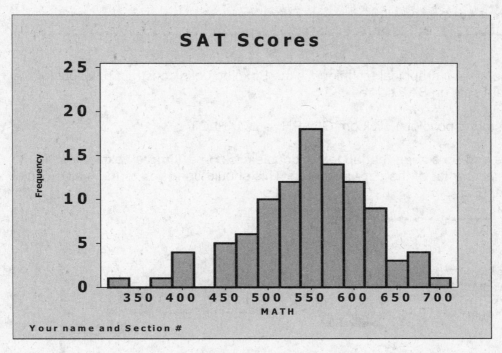

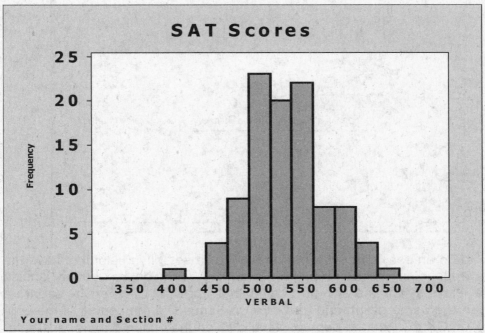

What do these two histograms tell you about the SAT Scores? First, you should notice the shapes. Both histograms appear to be rather mound-shaped. It also looks as if the center of the set of Math SAT scores is higher than the center of the set of Verbal SAT scores. The Verbal SAT scores appear to be more concentrated around the center, and the Math SAT scores seem to show more variation.

Boxplots

• •

Another useful graphical technique is the Boxplot. Let's construct boxplots for the two data sets on SAT scores.

To construct boxplots, click on: GRAPH → BOXPLOT

On the pop-up screen that appears, double-click on a **Simple** boxplot icon in the upper left corner of the pop-up screen. This should bring you to the main boxplot screen. (Fig. 2-3)

• •

Fig. 2-3

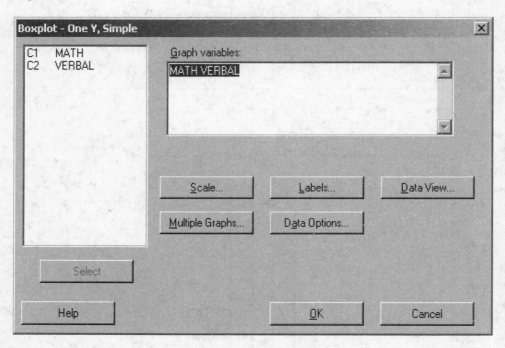

In order to do an easy comparison of the two data sets, it is helpful to have the boxplots appear on the same page. To do this, click on the button labeled **Multiple Graphs**. On the pop-up screen that appears, click on **In separate panels on the same graph** and also click on **Same Y** at the bottom of the pop-up. Click on OK to close the pop-up. Next, click on the button **Labels**, and enter a **title** of SAT SCORES and put your name and section number as a **Footnote**. Click on OK to close that Window and then click on OK again to produce the Boxplots. (Fig. 2-4)

Fig. 2-4

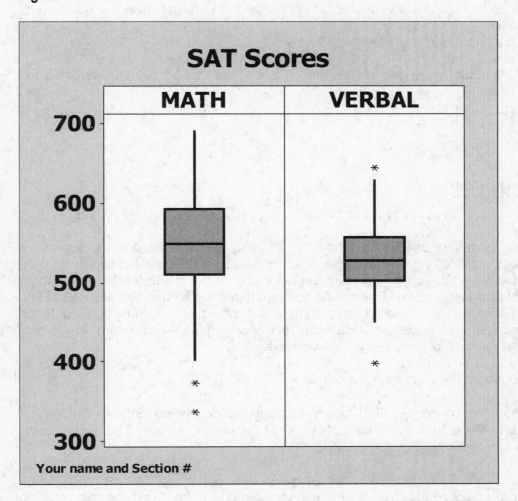

Each boxplot gives you a nice picture of the data set. The plot divides the data into four parts—the lower quartile, the upper quartile and the two middle quartiles. The box itself is drawn using the first quartile (Q1) as the bottom of the box and the third quartile (Q3) as the top of the box. Thus, the box itself represents the middle 50% of the data. The median is shown as a horizontal line drawn inside the box. If the median line is drawn through the middle of the box, then the middle 50% of the data set is evenly spread out on either side of the median. If the median line is closer to the bottom of the box, then the data points between Q1 and the median fall closer together and the points between the median and Q3 are more spread out. The lower 25% and the upper 25% of the data (with the exception of any outliers) are represented by the lines, called whiskers, which extend from the top and bottom of the box. The outliers are unusual values which are flagged with an asterisk (*) so that these points can be checked. MINITAB uses the following criteria for outliers:

A data point is considered an outlier if it is smaller than the *lower   inner fence*.

(The lower inner fence is Q1 - 1.5 * (Q1 - Q3).)

A data point is also considered an outlier if it is larger than the *upper inner fence*.

(The upper inner fence is Q3 + 1.5 * (Q1 - Q3).)

All unusual values should be verified to be sure that a data entry error did not occur.

Dotplots

• •

Dotplots are very useful when the data sets you have are small. Suppose we are interested in looking at the statistics for a Women's Collegiate Basketball team, and we have data on the number of points scored per game for the five starting players for last season. The data is contained in a file named **WOMENBB.MTW.** Open the file. You should have a data set with five columns of data (each column represents an individual player). To graphically compare the points scored for each player, we will use dotplots.

To construct the dotplots, click on: GRAPH→ DOTPLOT

On the pop-up screen that appears, double-click on the **Simple** dotplot for **Multiple Y's** icon in the lower left corner of the pop-up screen. This should bring you to the main dotplot screen. (Fig. 2-5)

In the window that appears, for **Graph Variables**, select all five columns. In order to compare the five players, it is very important that the dotplots are set up using the same scale. MINITAB does this automatically. Next, click on the **Labels** button, and enter an appropriate **Title** and enter your name and section number in the **Footnote** field, and then click on **OK**.

● ●

Fig. 2-5

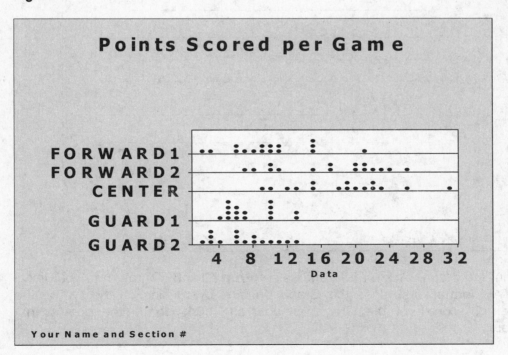

Click on OK to view the dotplots. (Fig. 2-6)

● ●

Fig. 2-6

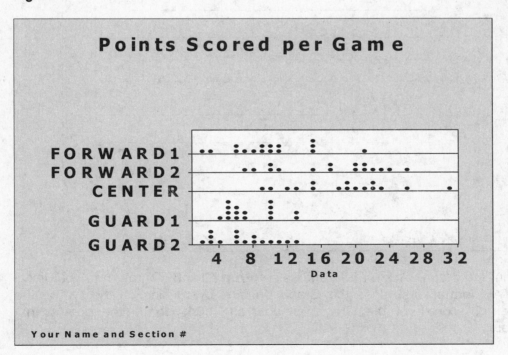

The default font used for the axis labels is too large in the above dotplots. To adjust the Y-axis font size, double-click on one of the labels. A pop-up screen will appear. Click on the **Font** tab, and select a **size** 8 font. Click OK. Repeat this process for the X-axis font. Also click on the **Scale** tab for the X-axis. Click on **Position of ticks** and enter 2 : 32 / 2. This tells MINITAB that you want a tick label from 2 to 32 in steps of 2. Click on OK to view the new plots. (Fig. 2-7)

These dotplots (Fig. 2-7) give you a quick and easy way of looking at the five players simultaneously. The dots represent the data points (points scored per game) for each game played by the player. The values along the X-axis represent the number of points scored, while the dots represent the number of times a player scored that many points. For example, the dotplot for Guard2 shows that she scored 2 points in one game—there is 1 dot above the 2 on the X-axis. Guard2 also scored 3 points in 3 games, 4 points in 1 game, 5 points in no games, 6 points in 3 games, 7 points in 1 game, etc. Since the scales are the same on all five plots, it is very simple to compare the points scored by each player.

• •

Fig. 2-7

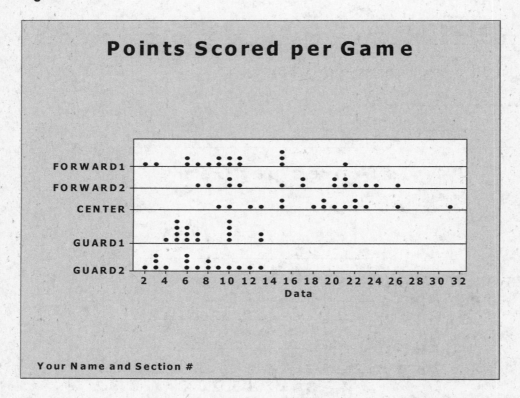

To print the graph, click on **File** and select **Print Graph.** To return to your initial MINITAB format, first close the Graph Window by clicking on the **"X"** in the upper right corner of the Graph Window and click **No** on the pop-up that appears.

Stem and Leaf Displays

•••

A stem-and-leaf display is the last of the graphical techniques that we will look at in this lesson. It is another way of getting a picture of the data set. It is different from the other graphs in that the stem-and-leaf display actually displays the raw data (in its original form or in a rounded form). In a stem-and-leaf the data is displayed in numerical order.

Let's begin by looking at a set of test scores from a midterm exam in an Elementary Statistics course with 50 students. To do this, open the file named **MIDTERM.MTW.** In your Data Window, you should have one column of data labeled SCORES. This is the data that you will use to construct the stem-and-leaf.

When constructing stem-and-leaf displays, the graphs will appear as part of the Session Window. When you complete this lesson and print your Session Window, the stem-and-leaf displays will be part of your printout.

Click on: GRAPH → STEM-AND-LEAF

In the window that appears, for **Graph Variables,** double-click on C1. Then click on **OK** to view the stemplot in the Session Window. You may have to **Maximize** your Session Window to see the entire stemplot. (Fig. 2-8)

A stem-and-leaf display is meant to give a quick overview of the data. It is not a sophisticated chart that you would see in magazines or newspapers. In the MINITAB display, the first column on the left is a counter. (This column counts the number of data points from the smallest value up to the median, and then counts down to the largest data value.) The stems are the next column of numbers. The leaves are the numbers to the right of the stems. The data itself is separated into these two parts: the stem and the leaf.

• •

Fig. 2-8

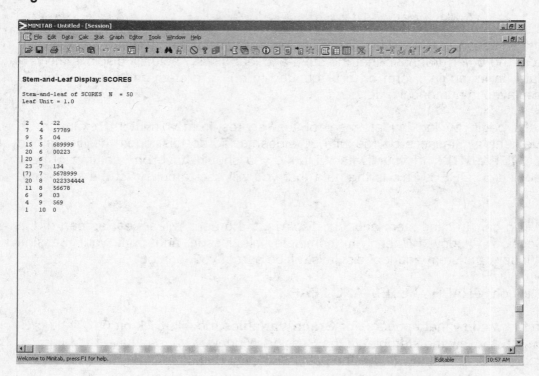

In this data set, notice that the stems range from 4 to 10. In the first row of the display you see: 4 22. This represents two data points: 42 and 42. *(Remember, ignore the first number in each row for now.)* The second row of the display represents five points: 45,47,47,48 and 49. (Notice that the counter on the left shows "7", which represents the total of seven data points that are contained in the first two rows of the display.) This stemplot gives a clear picture of the shape of the data, which appears to be bimodal.

Saving Graphs for Use in Word Files

Any graph produced in MINITAB can be saved and used in Word documents. This is very handy when you are preparing a report that includes graphs. It is easy to save a graph in some format other than MINITAB. The Graph Window must be active.

Click on FILE → SAVE GRAPH AS

A pop-up screen will appear. It will allow you to select where to save the graph and what format to save it as. At the bottom of the pop-up, click on the down arrow beside **Save as type:** to view the different types of formats that the graph can be saved in. Most of the types listed can be inserted in a Word document.

Assignment

• •

Please answer all questions in the space provided. When you have completed this assignment, tear the pages along the perforation. Include with this assignment all computer work that is required to answer the questions. Each graph must be labeled with a title, axis labels, and a footnote with your name and section number. If the assignment requires you to print the Session Window, click in the Session Window and type your name and section number so you can identify your printout.

1. For this example, you will use the file FINAL1.MTW. This large data set contains the final grades for two Introductory Statistics classes.

    a. Create a pair of histograms using the same scale. Be sure to label the graph with appropriate titles, footnotes, and axis labels. Maximize and print each histogram.

    b. Write a paragraph comparing and describing the two distributions of grades. Be sure to discuss shape (mound-shaped, skewed, bimodal), spread (max and min), and central tendencies.

2. For this example, you will use the file REBOUND1.MTW. This file contains the number of rebounds per game for five starting players on a leading Women's basketball team.

    a. Do a set of dotplots on the same scale to display the data.

b. Write a paragraph summarizing the data. Discuss similarities and differences among the players. Be sure to consider the positions played.

3. For this example, you will use the file BBSCORE1.MTW. The file contains points scored by the winners and by the losers and the point spread. (Notice that point spread equals Winning Score - Losing Score.) In this example, the winner is a particular Women's basketball team that was undefeated for an entire season, 35-0. The losers are the different opposing teams.

a. Construct a stem-and-leaf display of the point spread data (C3).

The stem ranges from _____ to _____.

What data values are represented by the second row of the stemplot? _____

Looking at the stemplot, you would conclude that for most games the point spread was between _____ and _____.

Looking at the stemplot, determine the number of games in which the point spread was less than 30 points? _____

Do any data points look like possible outliers? _____
Which ones? _____

b. Do a boxplot of C3 to see if the "possible outliers" actually appear as outliers. What did you discover?

c. From the boxplot, approximate the following data values:

Median _____
First quartile _____   Third quartile _____   IQR _____
Minimum data value _____
Maximum data value _____

d. Construct two boxplots on the same page to compare the points scored by the Winners, C1, to the points scored by the Losers, C2.

e. From the boxplot for the Winners, fill in the following information:

Highest Score _____   Lowest Score _____
First quartile _____   Third quartile _____   IQR _____

25% of the time, the Winners scored more than _____ points.

25% of the time, the Winners scored less than _____ points.

50% of the time, the Winners scored between 80 and _____ points.

f. From the boxplot for the Losers, fill in the following information:

75% of the time, the Losers scored fewer than _____ points.

One losing team did very well against the Winners. How many points did they manage to score? _____

Chapter 3

Measures of Central Tendency and Variation

THE GRAPHICAL METHODS for representing data that you studied in the previous lessons are very useful techniques for organizing data. As you have probably discovered, it is very difficult to get any useful information from a list of numbers. An organized display of the data set is much more informative. In addition to the graphical techniques, there are some basic measurements that can be calculated from the data set. These measurements describe the data set by using two key characteristics—central tendency and variation.

Central Tendency

One statistic that measures the center of a data set is the average or MEAN. Everyone is familiar with this measurement. It is calculated by adding all the data points in the set and dividing by the number of data points in the set. Another statistic that measures the center is the MEDIAN. The median divides the data set in half—50% of the data points have values less than or equal to the median and 50% of the data points have values greater than or equal to the median.

You might ask why there are two different measures of the center of a data set. To answer this question, let's create three small data sets. We will enter the data directly into a MINITAB worksheet.

In the Data Window, enter the following data points into Column 1:

1 2 3 4 5 6 7 8 9 10

Enter the following data points into Column 2:

1 2 3 4 5 6 7 8 9 25

Enter the following data points into Column 3:

1 2 3 4 5 6 7 8 9 100

Give each column a name by placing the cursor in the box directly below the column heading. Under C1 type "Trial 1"; under C2 type "Trial 2" and under C3 type "Trial 3". (Fig. 3-1)

• •

Fig. 3-1

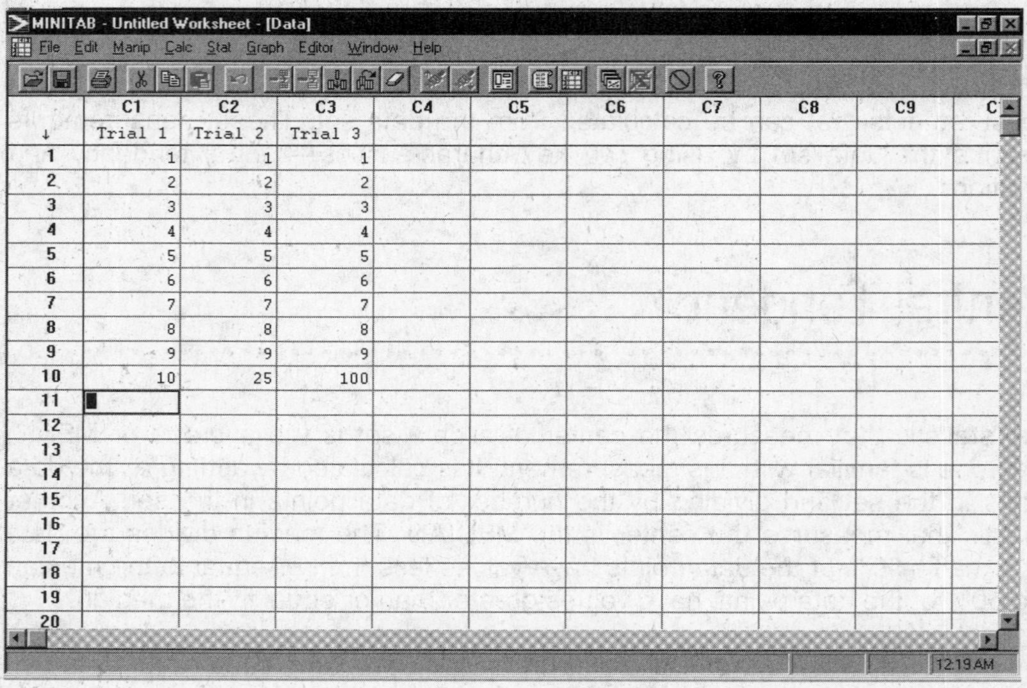

Let's compare the means and medians for these three columns. To do this, click on:

STAT → BASIC STATISTICS → DISPLAY DESCRIPTIVE STATISTICS

In the screen that appears, highlight all three columns and click on **SELECT.** These three columns will appear in the box entitled **VARIABLES.** Click on **OK.** (Fig. 3-2)

• •

Fig. 3-2

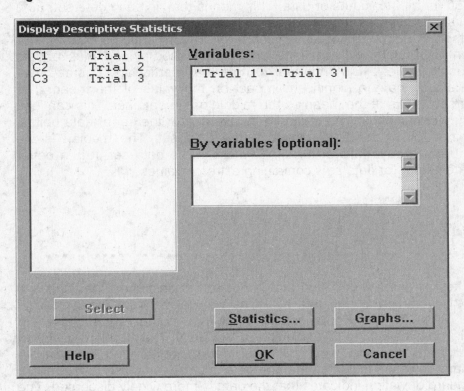

The following information should appear in the Session Window: (Fig. 3-3)

• •

Fig. 3-3

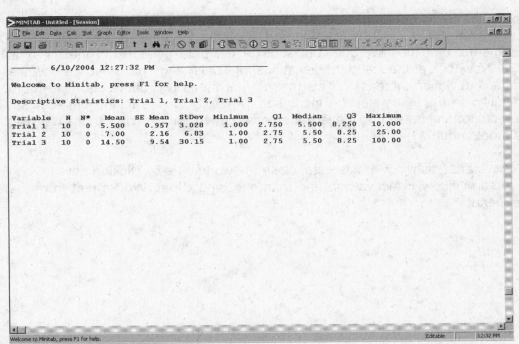

Notice the values of the mean and median for the three columns of data. The median is 5.50 for all 3 columns of data. This means that, in each data set, 50% of the observations are less than or equal to 5.50 and 50% of the observations are greater than or equal to 5.50. Now look at the mean. It jumps from 5.50 to 7.00 and then to 14.50. In each case the jumps are caused by one unusual data point (a probable outlier). It is important to note that, particularly in small data sets, an outlier can have a significant impact on the value of the mean. The "average" person thinks of the mean as the middle of the data set. This can lead to some misunderstandings. The mean is the average of the set of data points, but it might not fall at the 50 % mark of the data set. The median is the measurement that always falls at the 50 % mark in the data set. It is a better measure of the center for data sets containing extreme values.

Variation

The second key piece of information that is needed to describe a data set is a measure of the variation in the data set. One way to measure variation is to calculate the RANGE. The Range is: MAX - MIN. Another statistic used to calculate variation is called the STANDARD DEVIATION. The standard deviation is a measure of the "average" deviation of the data points around the mean. A "small" standard deviation indicates that the data is clustered close to the mean. A "large" standard deviation indicates that the data is more widely dispersed. The terms "large" and "small" are used in relation to the actual values in the data set. For example, a standard deviation of 100 would be considered "large" in a data set with a mean of 150. In a data set with a mean of 5000, a standard deviation of 100 would be considered "small."

Look at the Session Window (Fig. 3-3) that contains the Descriptive Statistics for Trial 1, Trial 2 and Trial 3. The standard deviation for the Trial 1 data is 3.028. This means that the "average" deviation of the data points from the mean is 3.028. Now look at the standard deviations for Trial 2 and Trial 3. Notice how the standard deviation increases. This means that these two data sets have more variability. In this example, the increased variability is due to the outliers. So, when comparing data sets, the larger standard deviation indicates that a data set has more variability.

Since we are finished with this data, close the worksheet by clicking anywhere in the Data Window to activate it, and then choosing **Close Worksheet** from the **File** menu.

Using the Mean and Standard Deviation
Empirical Rule: For Normally Distributed
Data
••

How can we make use of both the mean and standard deviation of a data set? We can combine these two key characteristics to get an idea of the distribution of the data. How we use these characteristics to describe the data set depends on the information we have regarding the shape of the data. If we use a histogram, stem-and leaf or dotplot to graph the data and see that the data is mound-shaped then we can make the following three statements (called the Empirical Rule) about the data set:

a. Approximately 68% of the data is contained in the interval $[\bar{x} \pm 1s]$

b. Approximately 95% of the data is contained in the interval $[\bar{x} \pm 2s]$

c. Approximately 100% of the data is contained in the interval $[\bar{x} \pm 3s]$.

As an example, let's look at the SAT.MTW data set. This data set contains MATH and VERBAL SAT scores. For this example, we will use the VERBAL scores. First, construct a histogram of the data, (GRAPH → HISTOGRAM). You should notice from your histogram that the data looks basically mound-shaped with no unusual values. Now that you have seen a display of the data set, close the Graph Window by clicking on the X in the upper right corner.

Find the mean and standard deviation of the data by using:

STAT → BASIC STATISTICS → DISPLAY DESCRIPTIVE STATISTICS

The mean is 530.67 and the standard deviation is 43.54.

The following steps are used to calculate the $[\bar{x} \pm 1s]$, $[\bar{x} \pm 2s]$, and $[\bar{x} \pm 3s]$ intervals in MINITAB. (A hand calculator can also be used for these calculations.) First, calculate the value for the lower limit: $[\bar{x} - 1s]$. To do this, click on:

CALC → CALCULATOR

In the screen that appears, you will **Store result in variable** C3. In the box for **Expression** type: 530.67 - 43.54. Click on **OK.** Your result, 487.13, should appear in C3. Now, calculate the value for the upper limit: $[\bar{x} + 1s]$. To do this, return to the Calculator screen. This time **store result in variable** C4, and the **Expression** is 530.67 + 43.54. Click on **OK.** Your result, 574.21, should appear in C4.

You can now use this information to make the following statement about the data:

"Approximately 68% of the Verbal SAT Scores fall between 487.13 and 574.21."

Now repeat the procedure to calculate $[\bar{x} - 2s]$ and $[\bar{x} + 2s]$. For $[\bar{x} - 2s]$, **store result in variable** C5, and type the **Expression:** 530.67 - 2*43.54. For $[\bar{x} + 2s]$, **store result in variable** C6 and type the **Expression:** 530.67 + 2*43.54. These numbers (in C5 and C6) represent the $[\bar{x} \pm 2s]$ interval and can be used in the following statement:

"Approximately 95% of the Verbal SAT scores lie between 443.59 and 617.75."

Finally repeat the procedure to calculate $[\bar{x} - 3s]$ and $[\bar{x} + 3s]$ and **store results in variable** C7 and C8. These numbers represent the $[\bar{x} \pm 3s]$ interval and can be used in the following statement:

"Approximately 100% of the Verbal SAT scores lie between 400.05 and 661.29."

Let's look at the data and see how well the Empirical Rule works. Determine how many data points actually do fall in the intervals that we created. Let's begin with the $[\bar{x} \pm 3s]$ interval and see how many data points are in this interval. It would be rather difficult to answer this question with the data as it appears in C2. It would be much easier to look at the data in numerical order. To do this, click on:

DATA → SORT

In the screen that appears, the **Sort column** is C2 Verbal and the **By Column:** is also C2 Verbal. (Note: MINITAB assumes the sort order is ascending unless you select the **descending** check box.) Below the heading **Store sorted data in,** select **Columns of current worksheet** and type in C9. (Fig. 3-4)

Fig. 3-4

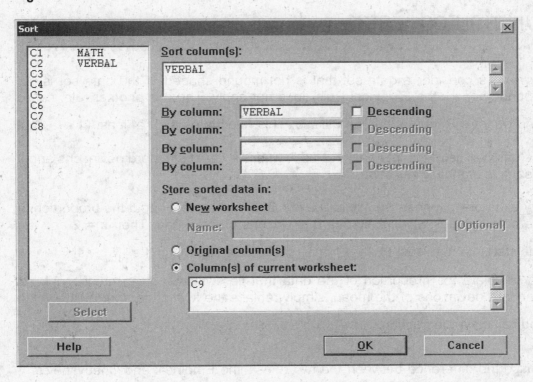

The Empirical Rule states that approximately 100% of the data lies between 400.05 and 661.29. Look through the ordered set of data (C9) by moving the down arrow on the right side of the Data Window. There is only one data point, 397, which falls outside the interval (400.05 - 661.29). So, the Empirical Rule is correct. (99% of the data falls within the interval and 99% is very close to 100%, which is what the Empirical Rule states).

How many data points fall outside the interval [$\bar{x}$ ± 2s], (443.59 - 617.75)? There are three points: 397, 629 and 645. So, 97 out of 100, or 97%, of the data actually lies within the [$\bar{x}$ ± 2s] interval. The Empirical Rule states that approximately 95% of the data should lie in this interval. So, the Empirical Rule's estimate is a good estimate of what actually did occur.

Lastly, how many points fall outside the interval [$\bar{x}$ ± 1s], (487.13 - 574.21)? There are 30 points: Data points numbered #1 - 14 and # 85 - 100. So 70% of the data is contained in the interval [$\bar{x}$ ± 1s]. Again, the Empirical Rule, which states that approximately 68% of the data should fall in the interval [$\bar{x}$ ± 1s], works well.

We have just verified the Empirical Rule by calculating the percentages of the sample data which fall within 1, 2, and 3 standard deviations of the mean. Using only the mean and standard deviation of a sample, the Empirical Rule can be used to describe the distribution of the whole population.

Chebyshev's Rule: For Non-normally Distributed Data

Now, let's consider a data set that is not mound shaped. If the data set is not mound shaped, the Empirical Rule does not apply. There is another rule, called Chebyshev's Rule that can be utilized. This rule states that "at least $(1 - \dfrac{1}{k^2})$ of the data will lie in the interval $[\bar{x} \pm ks]$", where k = # of standard deviations and s = sample standard deviation.

For example, suppose we would like to make a statement about the proportion of the data that lies within **2** standard deviations of the mean. Then **k = 2** and the rule states that at least $(1 - \dfrac{1}{2^2})$ or $\dfrac{3}{4}$ of the data lies within the $[\bar{x} \pm 2s]$ interval. To calculate the proportion of the data that lies within a given number (k) of standard deviations of the mean, simply replace the **k** with the appropriate value and calculate the fraction $(1 - \dfrac{1}{k^2})$.

Notice the difference between the two rules - the Empirical and Chebyshev's. If you look at the $[\bar{x} \pm 2s]$ interval, the Empirical Rule states that "approximately 95% of the data lies in that interval". Chebyshev's Rule states that "at least 75% of the data lies in that interval". It is important that you use the correct rule for the given data set. This can be determined by graphing the data. If the data appears relatively mound shaped, then the Empirical Rule should be used. If it does not look mound shaped, then Chebyshev's Rule should be used. Thus, using only the mean, the standard deviation and one of these rules, you can get a general idea of the interval in which you can expect most of your data to fall.

Close the Data Window since we are finished with this data.

Standardizing a Data Set

Often, when analyzing data, it is necessary to compare data sets that have different means and standard deviations. For example, suppose you want to compare EXAM 1 and EXAM 2 grades in an Introductory Statistics course. The data is stored in a file named STANDARD.MTW. Open this worksheet.

Find the mean and standard deviation for each set of Exam scores. To do this, click on:

STAT → BASIC STATISTICS → DISPLAY DESCRIPTIVE STATISTICS

In the window that appears select the **Variables** C1 and C2 and click on **OK.** Notice that the means and standard deviations differ for the two exams.

How can we compare the observations in the two data sets? One way to make comparisons is to standardize the data sets. Standardizing a data set is done by using the following formula:

$$Z = \frac{X - \overline{X}}{S}$$

Each observation, X, is converted to a standardized value, Z. To do this in MINITAB, click on:

$$CALC \rightarrow STANDARDIZE$$

In the screen that appears, the columns you are **standardizing** are C1 and C2 so select both of them as **Input columns. Store the results** in two empty columns, C3 and C4. The standardizing formula we are using is **Subtract mean and divide by standard deviation.** Make sure that the correct choice is selected at the bottom of the pop-up. (Fig. 3-5)

• •

Fig. 3-5

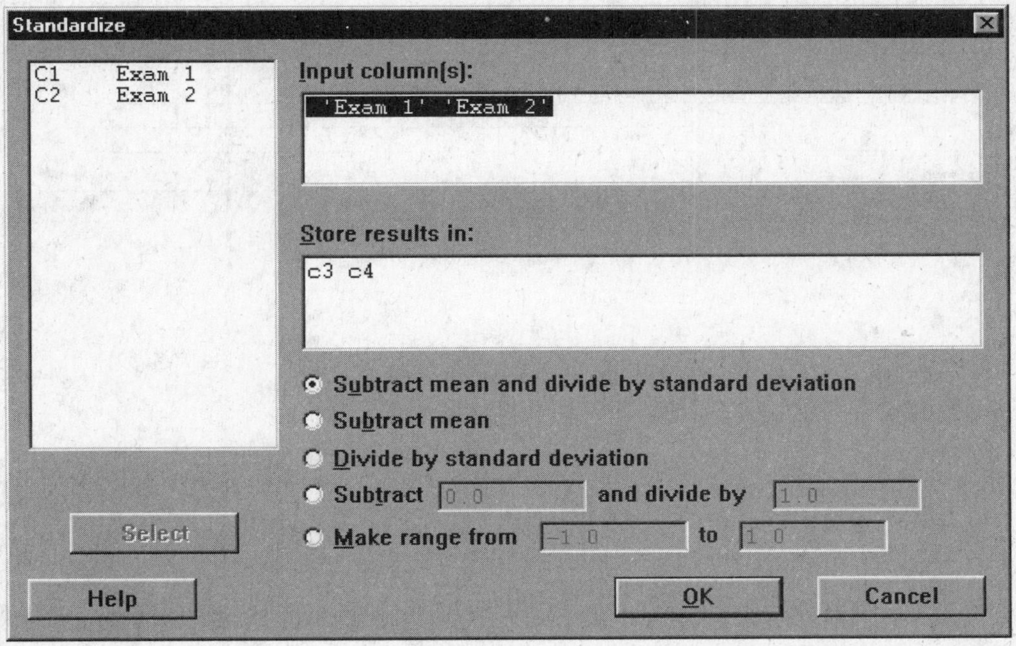

C3 and C4 now contain the standardized data. Standardized data sets all have the same mean (0.00) and the same standard deviation (1.00). Verify this for C3 and C4 by using:

STAT → BASIC STATISTICS → DISPLAY DESCRIPTIVE STATISTICS.

Now suppose that you are Person # 4 in the data set (Fig. 3-6). You scored 87 on the first exam and 80 on the second exam. On which of the two exams did you receive a higher grade relative to the rest of the class? To answer this question, look at your standardized scores of .22713 and .29580 (Fig. 3-6). The larger value indicates the higher score so your Exam 2 grade was actually better, relatively speaking.

● ●

Fig. 3-6

	C1	C2	C3	C4	C5	C6	C7	C8	C9	C
↓	Exam 1	Exam 2	Stand.1	Stand.2						
1	87	93	0.22713	0.94426						
2	100	80	0.88768	0.29580						
3	93	87	0.53200	0.64497						
4	87	80	0.22713	0.29580						
5	93	20	0.53200	-2.69709						
6	87	40	0.22713	-1.69946						
7	93	100	0.53200	1.29343						
8	100	80	0.88768	0.29580						
9	87	73	0.22713	-0.05337						
10	80	33	-0.12855	-2.04863						
11	80	100	-0.12855	1.29343						
12	73	87	-0.48424	0.64497						
13	100	87	0.88768	0.64497						
14	80	40	-0.12855	-1.69946						
15	87	73	0.22713	-0.05337						
16	80	93	-0.12855	0.94426						
17	87	20	0.22713	-2.69709						
18	80	67	-0.12855	-0.35266						
19	80	80	-0.12855	0.29580						
20	93	93	0.53200	0.94426						

Assignment ....

Please answer all questions in the space provided. When you have completed this assignment, tear the pages along the perforation. Include with this assignment all computer work that is required to answer the questions. Each graph must be labeled with a title, axis labels, and a footnote with your name and section number. If the assignment requires you to print the Session Window, click in the Session Window and type your name and section number so you can identify your printout.

1. For this example, you will use the file BASEBALL1.MTW. This file contains the 2004 salaries for two major league baseball teams. C1 contains the salaries for a randomly selected American League team, and C2 contains the salaries for a randomly selected National League team.

   a. Use MINITAB to calculate the mean, median and standard deviation for the salaries for each team.

AMERICAN LEAGUE	NATIONAL LEAGUE
Team:	Team:
Mean:	Mean:
Median:	Median:
Standard Deviation:	Standard Deviation:

   b. Which measure of central tendency, the mean or the median, do you think would give a more realistic picture of the salaries? Write an explanation justifying your choice.

   c. Use the means, medians and standard deviations of the two data sets to compare the two teams. Include comments on similarities and differences in salaries.

2. Construct a stem-and-leaf display of the salaries for the NL team.

    a. Describe the shape of the distribution of the salaries.

    b. Calculate the interval [$\bar{x} \pm 2s$]. Using the appropriate rule, Empirical or Chebyshev's, make a statement about the percentage of the players' salaries that you would expect to fall within this interval.

3. Suppose you are interested in determining how well the highest paid player is paid relative to the rest of the players on his team. For each team, convert all the players' salaries into standardized scores. Locate the highest paid player from each team.

    Highest AL salary:_____   Highest NL salary: _____

    Z-score: _____   Z-score: _____

    Compare the standardized scores for these two players. Who is the higher paid player relative to the rest of his team? Explain your conclusion.

4. For this example, you will use the COLLEGE1.MTW file. This file contains Verbal and Math SAT scores.

    a. Construct a histogram for the Math SAT scores. Be sure to include a title, X and Y axis labels, your name and your section.

    b. Describe the shape of the distribution.

    c. Calculate the mean and standard deviation of the Math scores.

    d. Calculate the intervals $[\bar{x} \pm 1s]$, $[\bar{x} \pm 2s]$, $[\bar{x} \pm 3s]$. What percentage of the data would you expect to fall within each of these intervals? (You can use MINITAB or a hand calculator to calculate the intervals.)

    e. Organize the data set into numerical order. What percentage of the data set actually did fall within the interval $[\bar{x} \pm 2s]$? List the data points that did not lie in the interval.

    f. Compare the means and standard deviations of the Math and Verbal SAT scores. On average, on which of the two parts of the SAT test do students do better? Which set of scores has more variability?

Chapter 4

Probability and Simulation

MATHEMATICAL MODELS have been used to describe real-world problems for centuries. Today, with the use of high speed computers, mathematical models have become more and more sophisticated and it is now possible to model very complex problems. We use mathematical models in statistics to describe random events, which are events whose outcomes vary. These models are called probability models or probability distributions.

A simple example of a random event is the roll of a die. When the die is rolled, the possible outcomes are the numbers 1 to 6. If the die is fair, each outcome is equally likely and has probability of $\frac{1}{6}$. This means that, even though any individual outcome is random, the long run outcome is predictable. This information can be displayed in a table, called a probability distribution, where X = the number rolled and P(X) = it's probability.

• •

Fig. 4-1

X	P(X)
1	.167
2	.167
3	.167
4	.167
5	.167
6	.167

The probabilities in the above table are theoretical probabilities. These probabilities are determined from the physical characteristics of the die. Since the die is fair, each of the sides has an equal chance of occurring so the probabilities in the above table are all the same.

Simulating Equally Likely Events
• •

We could also calculate experimental probabilities by "rolling" a fair die a large number of times. These experimental probabilities should closely agree with the probabilities in the theoretical model (Fig. 4-1).

Rather than actually rolling a die a large number of times, we will have MINITAB simulate the experiment. MINITAB will do this by randomly generating integers from 1 to 6 to represent the results of rolling a die. The random number generator will give each of the numbers, 1 to 6, an equal chance of occurring.

To do this, click on CALC → RANDOM DATA → INTEGER

In the screen that appears, **Generate** 100 rows, **Store in** C1, **Minimum value** is 1, **Maximum value** is 6. (Fig. 4-2)

• •

Fig. 4-2

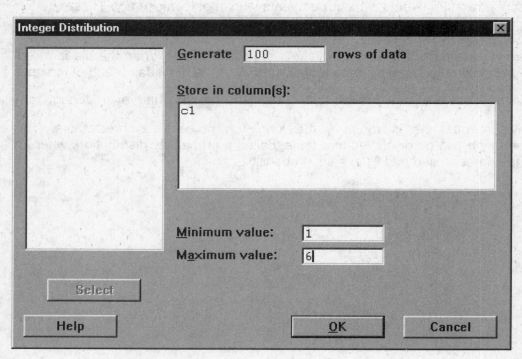

The results of 100 random rolls of a fair die are in C1 in the Data Window. Let's compare these experimental results with our theoretical model. To do this, we need to count the number of 1s, 2s, 3s, etc. that are in C1.

Click on: STAT → TABLES→ TALLY INDIVIDUAL VARIABLES

In the screen that appears, select the **Variable** C1 and **Display counts** and **percents** by selecting the boxes to the left of these options.

In the Session Window, a table of **Summary Statistics** will appear. This table lists the possible values of the random variable, X. In our example, the values are the numbers 1 through 6, representing the rolls of a die. The next column in the table is a count of the number of times, in 100 tosses, that the different outcomes occurred. The final column is the percent of times that the different outcomes occurred. If you try this experiment, your results will not be identical to the results in this table because each simulation is different. (Fig. 4-3)

● ●

Fig. 4-3

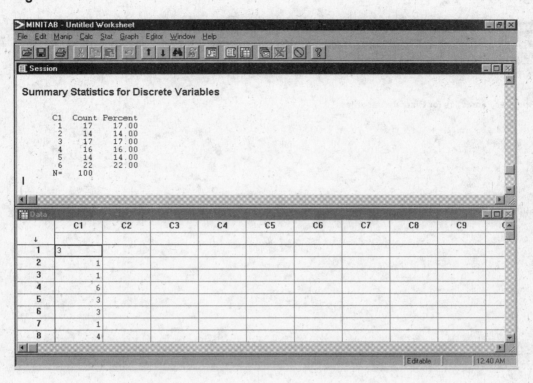

Compare the percentages in the Summary Table with the theoretical probabilities in Fig. 4-1. The theoretical probabilities and the experimental results should be close. As an example, look at the theoretical probability of rolling a "2" on a die. That's equal to .167. Now look at the experimental result for rolling a "2". In our example the result is 14% or .14. As you can see, these probabilities are not identical, but they are relatively close. The difference between them is due to randomness. An experiment with a limited number of trials (in this case, a limited number of rolls of the die), will not give the exact probabilities that are in the theoretical model.

The results of the experiment will tend to be closer to the theoretical model if the number of trials is increased. Let's see what happens if we roll a die 1000 times. Repeat the process using:

CALC → RANDOM DATA → INTEGER

Generate 1000 **rows** this time and **store results in** C2. Then create a new Summary Table. If you **Maximize** your Session Window and move the up arrow on the right side of your screen you can see the results of both experiments (Fig.4-4).

• •
Fig. 4-4

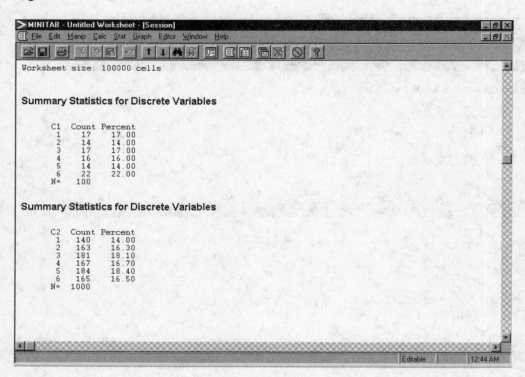

Notice that the probabilities in the larger experiment are closer to the theoretical probabilities.

Simulating Events That Are Not Equally Likely
• •

Suppose that the die we are using is a "loaded" die. The die is loaded so that a "1" will occur 50% of the time and the remaining 5 numbers will each occur 10% of the time. Simulating this experiment requires the use of a probability distribution because these events do not have equal probability. (In the previous example, when MINITAB generated the numbers 1 to 6, each number had an equal chance of occurring.)

The probability model for this experiment is the following:

• •

Fig. 4-5

X	P(X)
1	.500
2	.100
3	.100
4	.100
5	.100
6	.100

To simulate this in MINITAB, we need to enter the probability distribution into the Data Window.

Let's begin by clearing the Data Window. To do this, move the cursor to any location in the Data Window. Click on: EDIT → SELECT ALL CELLS
Now all the data should be highlighted. Press the **Delete** key on your keyboard, and the Data Window should be empty. Using the probability model in Figure 4-5, enter the values of the random variable, X, in C1 and enter the theoretical probabilities in C2. Label C1 as "X" and C2 as "P(X)". (Fig. 4-6)

• •

Fig. 4-6

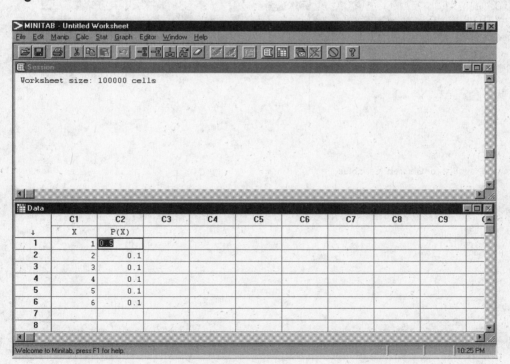

Now simulate rolling this "loaded" die 100 times. To do this, click on:

CALC → RANDOM DATA → DISCRETE

In the screen that appears, **Generate** 100 **rows of data**, **Store in columns** C3, **Values in** C1 and **probabilities in** C2. Click on **OK.**

What appears in C3 in the Data Window are the results of 100 rolls of a loaded die. Let's again compare these experimental results with our theoretical model. To do this, we need a summary of the results in C3.

To do this, click on: STAT → TABLES → TALLY INDIVIDUAL VARIABLES

Compare the theoretical probabilities (Fig. 4-5) in the model to your experimental results in your Session Window (Fig. 4-7). How close are they?

Now repeat the process again for 1000 "rolls" of the die. Notice that the experimental probabilities (Fig. 4-7) are closer to the theoretical probabilities. (Fig. 4-5) Since this is random data, your results will not be exactly the same as those shown below.

• •

Fig. 4-7

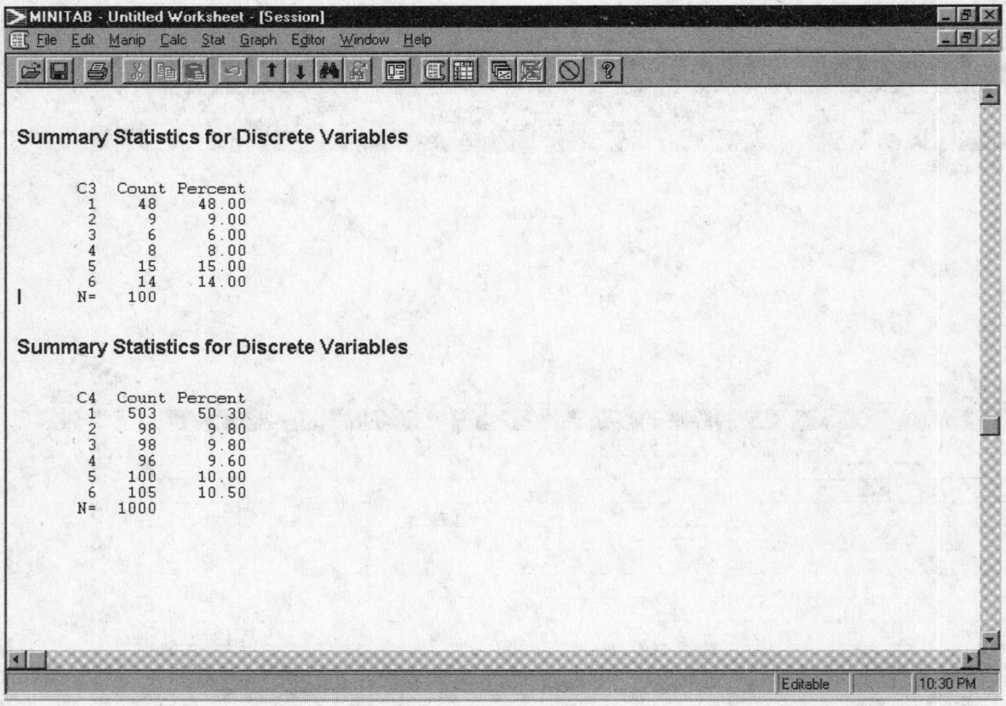

Chapter 5

The Binomial Random Variable

Y OU HAVE LEARNED that a random variable is a variable with a probability distribution associated with its set of possible outcome values. Some random variables have special names such as the BINOMIAL random variable and are well worth studying because knowledge of their probability distribution allows you to make important statistical inferences about a population based on a sample from this population.

The binomial random variable is one of the most important of all the random variables. Can you define what you mean when you say X is a binomial random variable? First of all, you must have a series of random trials (they are called binomial trials) satisfying all of the following conditions:

1. There are a fixed number of trials (n = number of trials).
2. All trials are independent.
3. There are two outcomes on each trial (success or failure).
4. There is a fixed probability of success on each trial
    (p = prob. of success).

If you let X = number of successes in n binomial trials, then X is a binomial random variable defined by the parameters n and p, where n is the number of trials and p is the probability of success on a trial.

For example, suppose we know that currently 22% of all adults in the U.S. smoke. Then p = .22 represents the proportion of individuals in the population who smoke. Also, p could be interpreted as the probability that a randomly selected individual smokes.

There are 3 important things that you will learn to do using MINITAB and the Binomial distribution:

1. If an experiment meets the conditions of a binomial model, then the model can be used to measure the likelihood (probability) of different outcomes. The back of your textbook has only a few selected binomial tables in which you can find these probabilities. We can use MINITAB to calculate any binomial probability that we want. There are two ways to do this:

    a. Using the probability distribution option, MINITAB can calculate P(X=b), where b is a constant. This probability can be viewed in the Session Window, or saved in a column.
    b. Using the cumulative probability distribution, MINITAB can calculate P(X ≤ b), where b is a constant. Again, this can be viewed in the Session Window or saved in a column.

2. A binomial distribution is a *discrete* distribution. Therefore, the appropriate graph to use for this distribution is a bar chart. The important thing to notice is the shape of the distribution. Recall that a binomial random variable is defined by n (number of trials) and p (probability of success). It is these two parameters that determine the shape of the distribution. Using MINITAB, we will produce the probability distribution, and then graph it.

3. There is a difference between the theoretical probability distribution and the experimental probabilities derived from a random sample. Many times we use sample results to estimate the probability that an event will or will not occur. We can compare experimental to theoretical probabilities by taking some random samples and creating a relative frequency table. The relative frequencies are the estimates of the theoretical probabilities. Using MINITAB, we will create random samples and relative frequencies so that we can make the comparison between these experimental probabilities and the theoretical probabilities of the model.

The following are some examples that demonstrate how to use MINITAB to do the three things listed above.

A. Suppose you would like to look at a binomial probability table for $n = 15$ and $p = .65$. Since your text does not have a binomial table for $p = .65$, you may produce a table in MINITAB as follows.

First, you must enter your X values in C1. These X values represent the number of successes in n trials. We know that the possible X values are 0,1,2,. . . n. In this case, n=15. A simple way to do this is to let MINITAB generate the numbers for you.

Click on:

CALC → MAKE PATTERNED DATA → SIMPLE SET OF NUMBERS

In the screen that appears, you want to:

Store patterned data in: C1
From first value: 0
To last value: 15
In steps of: 1

When these are filled in, click on **OK.** (Fig. 5-1). The numbers 0 through 15 should now be stored in C1.

• •
Fig. 5-1

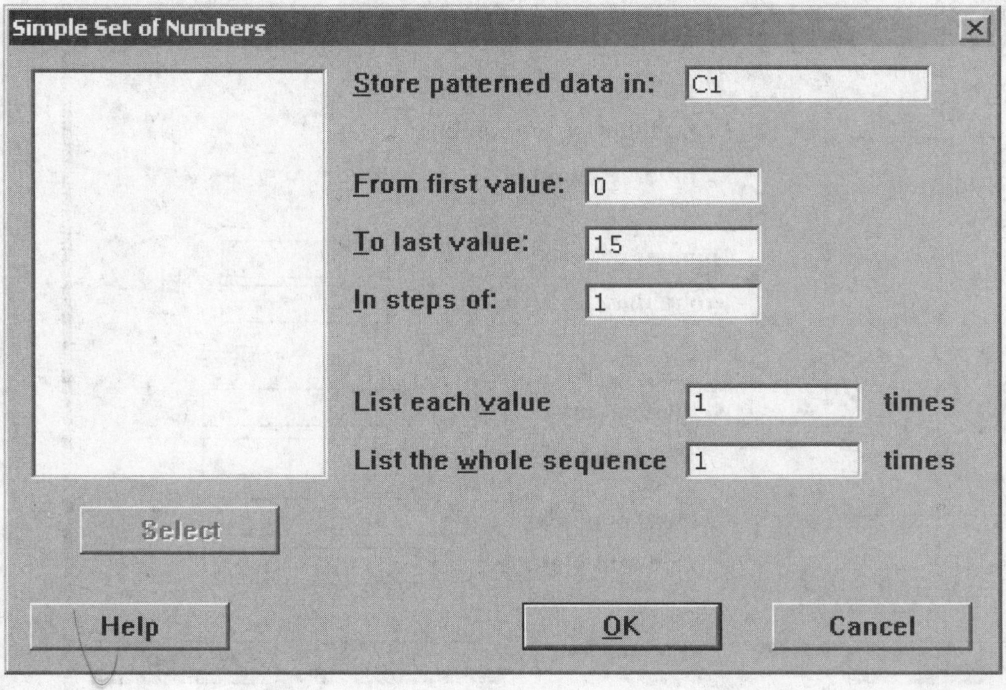

B. Next, create the binomial probabilities. Click on:

CALC → PROBABILITY DISTRIBUTIONS → BINOMIAL.

On the screen that appears, select **PROBABILITY**. Then fill in the following:

    Number of trials: 15
    Probability of success: .65
    Input column: C1
    Optional storage: (leave blank)

When you click on **OK**, (Fig. 5-2), the probability distribution table will appear in the Session Window because you left **OPTIONAL STORAGE** blank. If you want to save the probabilities (as you will for a graph), you can fill in an **OPTIONAL STORAGE** column, such as C2. If you do this, the probabilities will now be stored in C2.

• •

Fig. 5-2

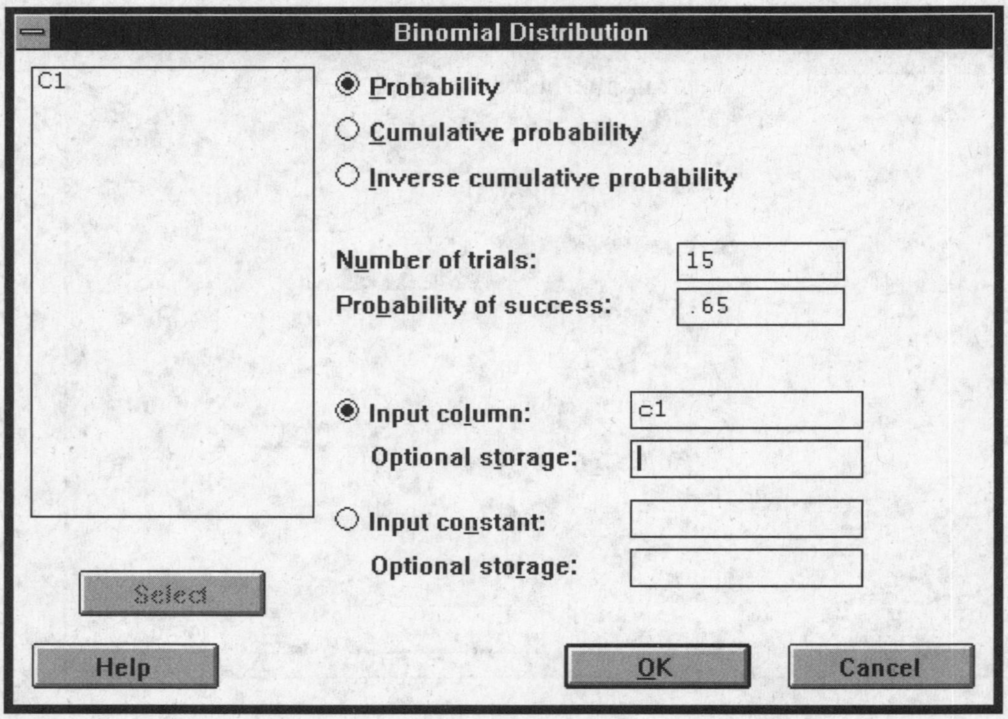

You may decide that rather than printing the entire probability table, you only want to find a specific probability. This is very simple to do. Use the same procedure as above, but this time leave **INPUT COLUMN** blank, and fill in **INPUT CONSTANT** with the desired X value. For example, to find P(X = 10), the **input constant** would be 10. Also, you will probably want to leave the **OPTIONAL STORAGE** blank so that the P(X=10) will be displayed in the Session Window. (When you try this, you should see P(X=10)=.2123) (Fig. 5-3)

You can also find the cumulative probability, which gives P(X ≤ c) where c is a value you choose. To do this, simply click on **CUMULATIVE PROBABILITY** (instead of PROBABILITY) on the Binomial Input Screen. All the other options work exactly as explained above. For example, if your input constant is 5, then you will see in the Session Window P(X ≤ 5) = .0124. (Fig. 5-3)

Fig. 5-3

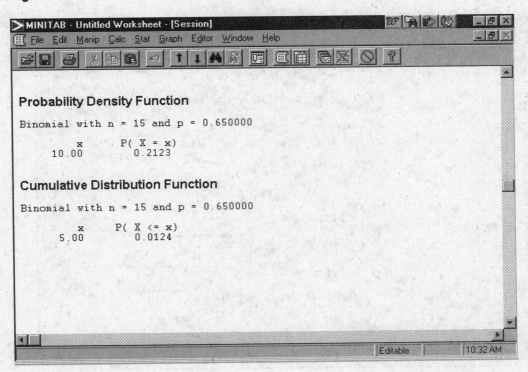

You can also use the **CUMULATIVE PROBABILITY** to find P(X >c) by finding P(X ≤ c) and subtracting it from 1. For example, P(X > 5) = 1 - P(X ≤ 5) = 1 - .0124.

C. Now suppose you would like to graph a binomial probability distribution to see its shape. We will use a bar chart to graph a binomial distribution. You can practice using a binomial with n=10 and p=.7. You'll need to create and save the X values in C1 (X = 0,1,…,10) and the probability distribution in C2, as explained in parts A and B above. Be sure to use the **optional storage** in C2. (Fig. 5-4)

• •
Fig. 5-4

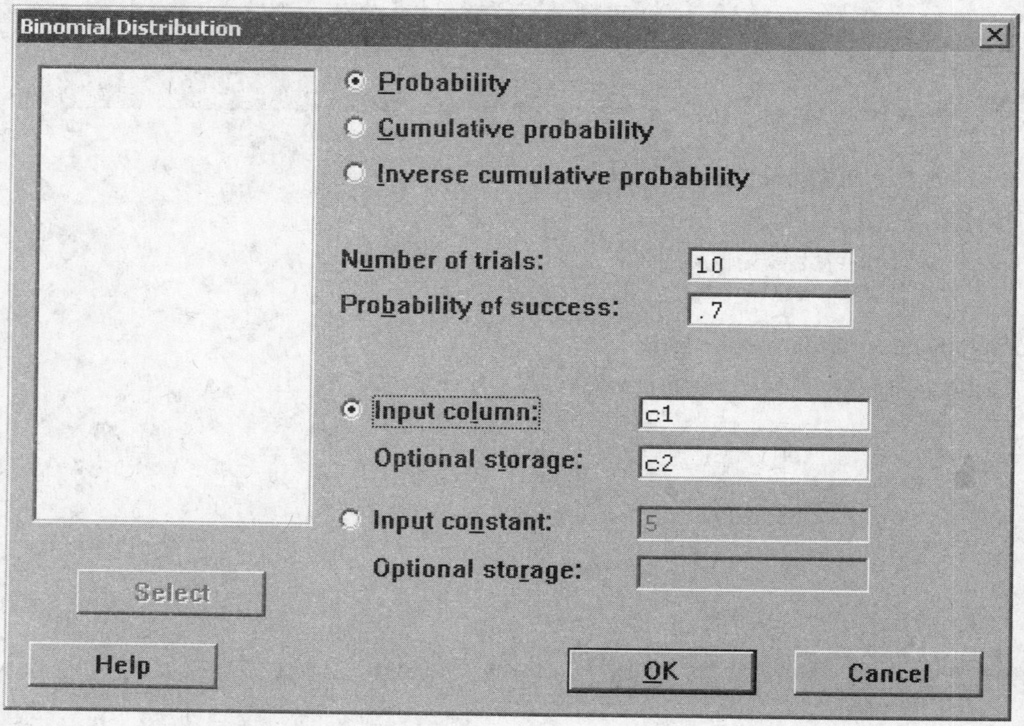

The Data Window should now have two columns filled. Name C1 "X", and C2 "P(X)". (Fig. 5-5)

• •
Fig. 5-5

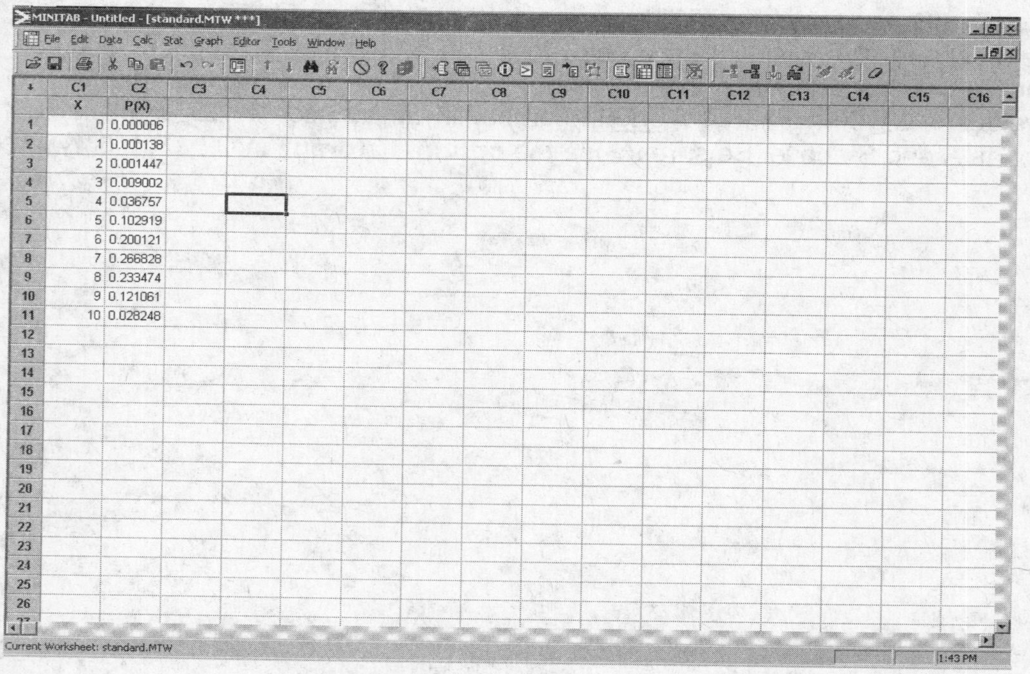

Now to create a bar chart, click on: GRAPH → BAR CHART

On the pop-up screen, the **Bars represent: values from a table.** Select a **Simple** bar chart and click on OK. You will be at the main bar chart screen. The **Graph variable** is C2, where the probabilities are stored. The **Categorical variable** is C1, where the X values are stored. Be sure to click on the **Labels** button and add a **Title** to your graph which indicates which binomial distribution it is (i.e. Binomial n=10, p=.7), and a **Footnote** with your name and section number. Click on OK to view the bar chart. (Fig. 5-6)

• •
Fig. 5-6

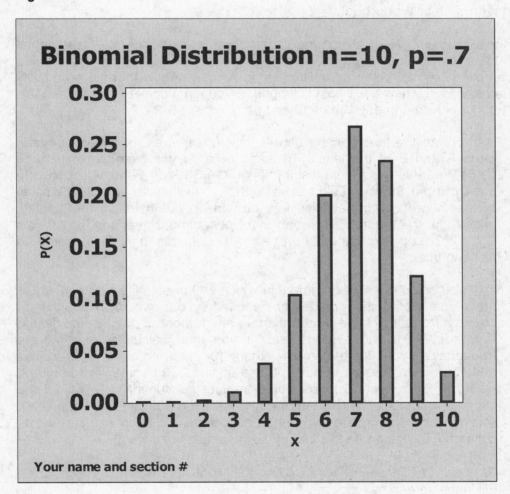

Assignment

••

Please answer all questions in the space provided. When you have completed this assignment, tear the pages along the perforation. Include with this assignment all computer work that is required to answer the questions. Each graph must be labeled with a title, axis labels, and a footnote with your name and section number. If the assignment requires you to print the Session Window, click in the Session Window and type your name and section number so you can identify your printout.

Begin with a clear worksheet.

1. In this problem, you will compare theoretical probabilities to experimental probabilities obtained using relative frequencies. You will use a coin flipping example since everyone is familiar with it. All of us know that the probability of a head is .5 when a fair coin is flipped. If you flip a coin 10 times, then this is a binomial experiment with n=10 and p=.5.

    a. First, create the theoretical probability distribution, as explained above in parts A and B of the lesson. (Please note: in this example, n=10 and p=.5) Print this theoretical distribution in the Session Window (by leaving the **Optional Storage** field blank) so that you will have an output display of the theoretical probabilities for comparison purposes. In the display, notice that the theoretical probability of observing 3 heads in the 10 flips is 0.1172. Your experimental probability of 3 heads in 10 flips should be close to this.

    b. Next, you *could* run an experiment in which 200 people flip a coin 10 times each and record the number of heads they observe. You could then create a frequency table by counting up the number of people who flipped 0 Heads, 1 Head, 2 Heads, etc. If you then calculated the relative frequencies, you could compare them to the theoretical probabilities printed in your Session Window. Since finding 200 people who would be willing to flip a coin 10 times would be time consuming, you will let the computer simulate the experiment by generating 200 random samples of size 10, and storing the number of successes for each sample in one column. First, generate the 200 random samples of size 10.

    Click on: CALC → RANDOM DATA → BINOMIAL
    Fill in the screen as follows:

    > **Generate** <u>200 </u>**Rows of Data**
    > **Store in column(s)**: C1
    > **Number of Trials**: 10
    > **Probability of Success**: .5

4. The shape of the graph of a binomial distribution depends on the value of both n and p. To see how the shape changes for a fixed value of n, you will let p vary and graph each probability distribution. Let X be a binomial random variable with n=10.

   a. For p = .18, .47, and .88, obtain the binomial probability distribution and a bar chart of each distribution. (Be sure to hand the graphs in with your assignment.)

   b. For small values of p, the binomial distribution is skewed to the _____.

      For large values of p, the binomial distribution is skewed to the _____.

      For values of p near _____ the binomial distribution is nearly symmetric.

5. Now see what happens when you hold p constant and vary n. Let X be a binomial random variable with p=.24.

   a. Obtain the probability distribution and graph of the distribution for both n=5 and 20.

   b. Describe the shape of each graph. (Skewed right, skewed left, symmetric?)

   c. As n increases, the probability distribution becomes more _____ in shape.

6. A Student Senate at a large university is made up of 60 students chosen to represent the entire student body. 20% of the students at this university are minorities. When the members of the senate are selected, only two members are minority students. The Minority Caucus claims that this Senate is racially biased. They decide to use statistics to prove their claim.

   a. Let X be the number of minority students who are selected for the senate. Does this meet the criteria of a binomial experiment? _____

      If so, what is n? _____

      What is p? _____

   b. Calculate the probability of the Senate being made up of so few minority students purely by chance. That is, find P(X ≤ 2) for this binomial problem.

c. Based on your answer to part b, would you be surprised if the senate had only 2 minority members? _____

Do you think the Minority Caucus is reasonable in their complaint of under-representation? _____

Explain.

d. Assuming that the senate represents the entire student body, how many minority students would you *expect* to be selected for the senate? _____

e. Use your calculator to calculate the standard deviation of the number of minority students selected. _____

f. Now suppose that the Student Senate has 9 minority students. Could the Minority Caucus make a case for racial bias in this case? Explain your answer using the Empirical Rule.

Chapter 6

The Normal Random Variable

A NORMAL RANDOM VARIABLE is one that follows a bell-shaped probability distribution. In class, you have learned to calculate a normal probability by first standardizing and then looking up the Z in the standard normal table in your textbook. In this lab, you will be doing the same type of problems, but you will be using MINITAB to calculate the probabilities. MINITAB calculates the probabilities directly, so there is no need to standardize or to use the standard normal table. Thus, you will be doing the same types of manipulations and calculations of the normal distribution as you have already done by hand, but you will be learning to work with the MINITAB program and finding how simply these problems can be solved with a computer.

In this lab, you will solve two types of problems using the normal random variable. You will also plot normal distributions with different means and standard deviations.

Normal Probability Problems

For the first type of problem, you will be given the mean and standard deviation for a normal random variable, X. You will then be asked to calculate probabilities such as $P(X \leq k_1)$, $P(X \geq k_2)$ or $P(k_1 \leq X \leq k_2)$ where k_1 and k_2 are given.

For example, if X is a normal random variable with $\mu = 100$ and $\sigma = 20$, what is the probability that an observed value of X will be less than 90?

To do this in MINITAB, click on:

CALC → PROBABILITY DISTRIBUTIONS → NORMAL

In the next window, select **CUMULATIVE PROBABILITY**. (Cumulative probability 'accumulates' all probability to the left of the input constant.) Enter the values for the mean and standard deviation. In this example, the **mean** is 100 and the **standard deviation** is 20. Next select **INPUT CONSTANT** by highlighting the circle to the left and then enter the value 90 in the box to the right of **INPUT CONSTANT**. Click on **OK**. (Fig. 6-1)

• •

Fig. 6-1

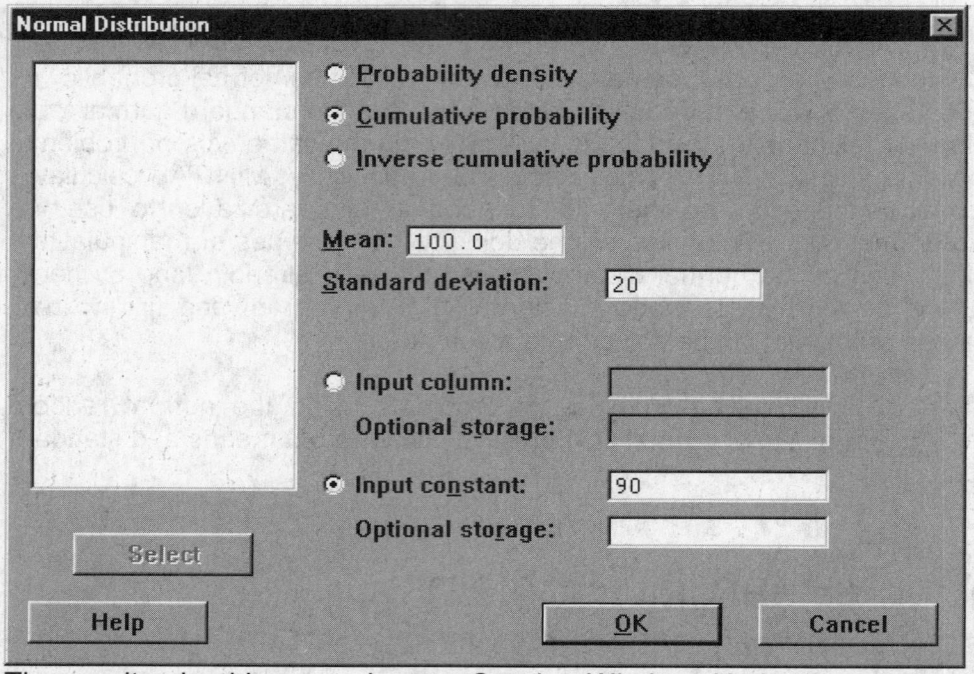

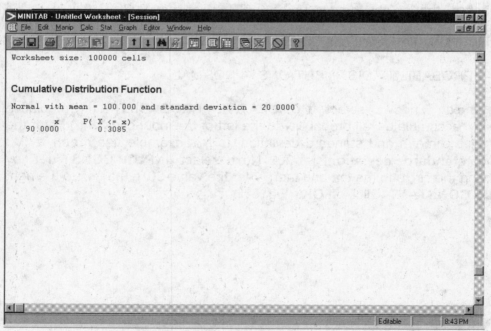

The results should appear in your Session Window. Under the column headed P(X ≤ x) you should see 0.3085. This is the probability that the random variable, X, takes on values less than or equal to 90. Thus,   P(X ≤ 90) = .3085. (Fig. 6-2)

• •

Fig. 6-2

In the space below, draw a normal curve by hand and shade in the area you wanted to calculate and label the area with the appropriate value. In this example, the label should be the value 0.3085.

Now suppose you wish to calculate $P(X \geq 130)$ using the same normal probability model with $\mu = 100$ and $\sigma = 20$. Use the same set of commands:

CALC $\rightarrow$ PROBABILITY DISTRIBUTIONS $\rightarrow$ NORMAL

This time, the **INPUT CONSTANT** is 130 (instead of 90). Notice your results give $P(X \leq 130) = .9332$ since cumulative probability always gives you the area <u>less</u> than the value entered (Fig. 6-3). Since you want the $P(X \geq 130)$, the answer you want is the complement of what MINITAB calculated. So, take the MINITAB result for this example and subtract it from 1 to get your answer. In the space below draw a normal curve and shade in the area you are interested in finding. You should label the area on the graph appropriately. (The answer is 1 - 0.9332 = 0.0668)

Now suppose you wish to calculate the probability that X is between 95 and 135 using the same probability model. This requires two separate Cumulative Probability calculations: one for $P(X \leq 135)$ and the other for $P(X \leq 95)$ (Fig. 6-3). You can then obtain the answer to this problem by subtracting the two probabilities. After obtaining the two probabilities from the Session Window, do the subtraction (0.9599 - 0.4013 = 0.5586), and then draw the normal curve in the space below. Shade in the appropriate area and label it with the correct probability value.

Fig. 6-3

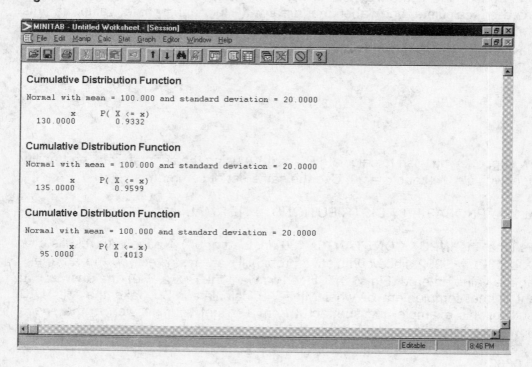

Inverse Normal Probability Problems

The second type of problem is called an Inverse Normal Problem. In this type of problem you are given that X is a Normal random variable with a specific mean and standard deviation. Then, you are asked to find the value, k, that is the cut-off point for a given percentage of the values of the random variable X. You did this in your textbook, but it was a complicated task to "un-standardize" and find the value of X. You probably used the equation, $X = \mu + Z\sigma$ to solve this type of problem in your textbook. Luckily, this is very simple to do using MINITAB.

For example, suppose X is a normal random variable with μ = 100 and σ = 20. What value of X marks the lower 20% of the distribution? (Thus, find the 20th percentile.)

To do this, the MINITAB commands are:

CALC → PROBABILITY DISTRIBUTION → NORMAL

In the next window, select **INVERSE CUMULATIVE PROBABILITY**. Enter the values of the mean and standard deviation. For this type of problem, the **INPUT CONSTANT** will be the area, a decimal number between 0 and 1. In the example we are using, the **INPUT CONSTANT** is .20. (Since 20% of the area is to the left of the value we are looking for.) Click on **OK**. (Fig. 6-4)

• •
Fig. 6-4

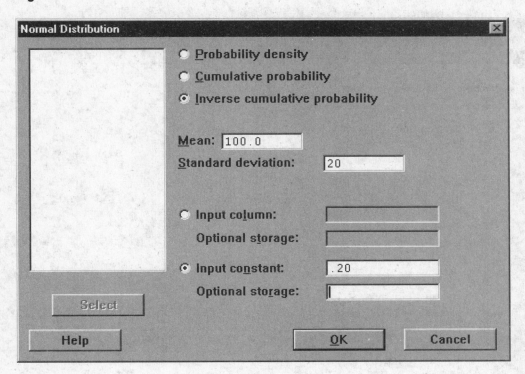

The answer appears in the Session Window under the column labeled 'X'. For this example, the answer is 83.1676 (Fig 6-5). This means that for the normal probability distribution with $\mu = 100$ and $\sigma = 20$, 20% of the data lies below the value 83.1676. Draw the normal curve, shade in the lower 20% and mark the value 83.1676 under the curve.

● ●

Fig. 6-5

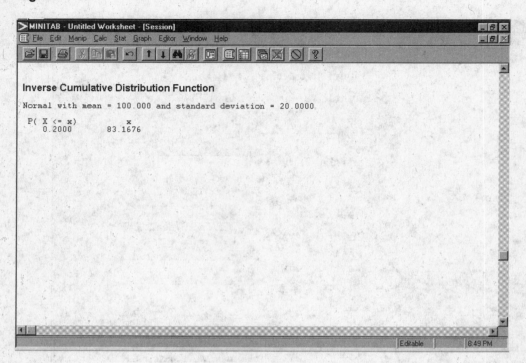

Consider the following problem: If X is a normal random variable with μ = 100 and σ = 20, what is the X-value that will mark off the upper 20% of the probability? Since MINITAB always calculates P(X $\leq$ some value), you must ask for an Inverse Cumulative Probability of 80%, since the point that marks the top 20% is the same point that marks the lower 80%. So, follow the same steps as in the previous example and simply change the **INPUT CONSTANT** to .80. In the Session Window, your answer should be 116.8324. Draw the curve and label it appropriately.

The last type of problem is the following. Suppose X is a Normal random variable with μ = 100 and σ = 20. What values of X mark off the central 80% of the distribution? If you mark off the central 80%, the remaining 20% will be divided evenly into 10% in each tail of the distribution. Thus, in the lower tail there is 10% below the value and in the upper tail there is 10% above the value. You need to calculate two **INVERSE CUMULATIVE PROBABILITIES**. For the lower tail, use an **INPUT CONSTANT** of .10 and for the upper tail, use an **INPUT CONSTANT** of .90. (Recall, the top 10% point is the same as the lower 90% point). Your two X-values are 74.3690 and 125.6310. This means that 80% of the data lies between these two values. Draw the curve and label it appropriately.

Graphing a Normal Curve

To graph a normal curve by hand is a simple task, and yet it takes a little thought to really understand the difference between two normal distributions. You know that the normal distribution is centered around its mean, and that most of its area falls within three standard deviations of the mean. MINITAB can draw a normal distribution quite easily, and can demonstrate the difference between two normal distributions. For example, suppose we want to compare a normal distribution with $\mu = 50$ and $\sigma = 5$ to a normal distribution with $\mu = 40$ and $\sigma = 5$. To do this in MINITAB, you first have to store some X values in C1 and the corresponding probabilities in C2. Since most all of the probability falls within 3σ of μ, our first distribution should fall within the interval $50 \pm 3(5)$, which is 35 to 65. Our second should fall within the interval $40 \pm 3(5)$, which is 25 to 55. To do this in MINITAB, we will first store X values for each distribution. We will put X values between 35 and 65 in C1, and X values between 25 and 55 in C3. After this is done, we will store normal probabilities for each distribution in C2 and C4. Lastly, we will plot the two distributions on the same graph.

Click on: CALC $\rightarrow$ MAKE PATTERNED DATA $\rightarrow$ SIMPLE SET OF NUMBERS

Fill in: **Store Patterned Data In**: C1
             From first value: 35
             To last value: 65
             In steps of: 1 (Fig. 6-6)

The above information is for the first distribution. Repeat the process for the second distribution, but store the data in C3. Use 25 as the first value and 55 as the last value.

• •
Fig. 6-6

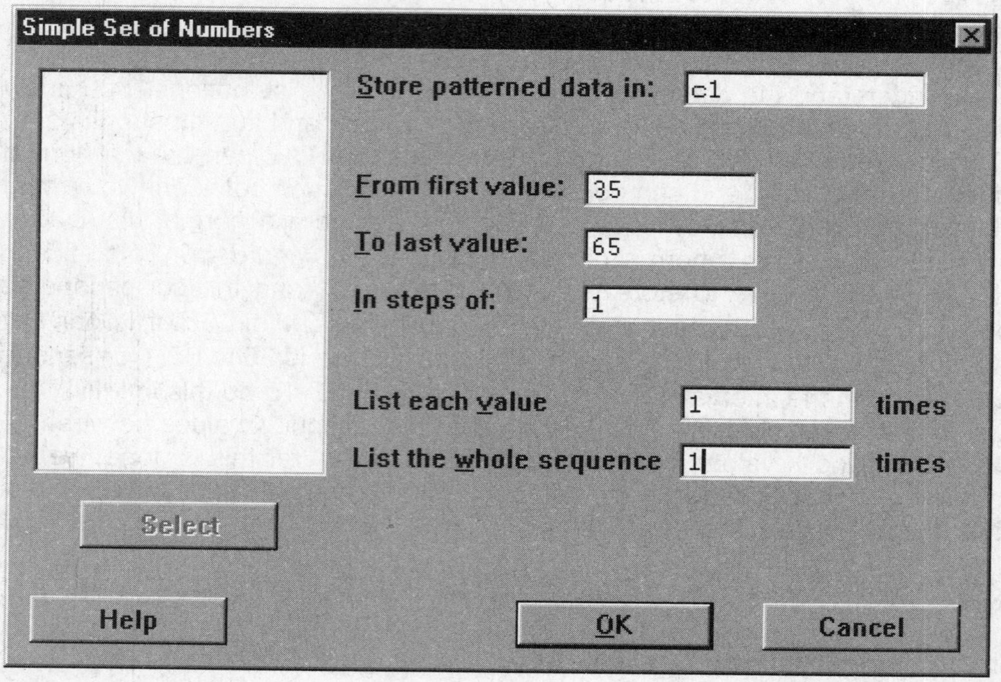

Next store the probabilities.

CALC → PROBABILITY DISTRIBUTION → NORMAL

Fill in:

    Probability Density (Be sure to select Probability Density)
    Mean: 50
    Standard Deviation: 5
    Input Column: C1
    Optional Storage: C2 (Fig. 6-7)

Repeat the process for the second distribution. This time $\mu=40$ and $\sigma=5$. The Input Column is C3 and the Optional Storage is C4.

• •
Fig. 6-7

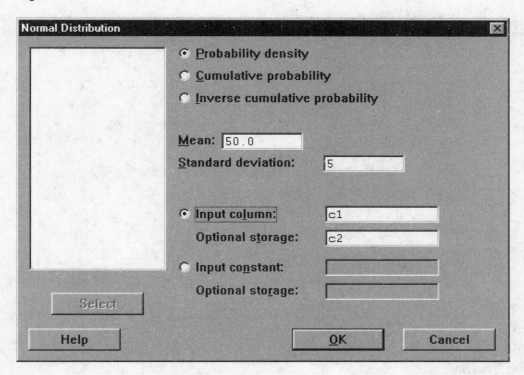

Now do the graphing. We will graph both normal curves on the same page so that we can compare the two distributions.

Click on: GRAPH → SCATTERPLOT

On the pop-up screen, select the plot icon **With Connect and Groups** and click OK to view the main plot window. In the input screen, the **Y variables** are the probabilities contained in C2 and C4. The **X variables** are the X-values contained in C1 and C3. Click on the check box to select **X-Y pairs form groups.** (Fig. 6-8)

Fig. 6-8

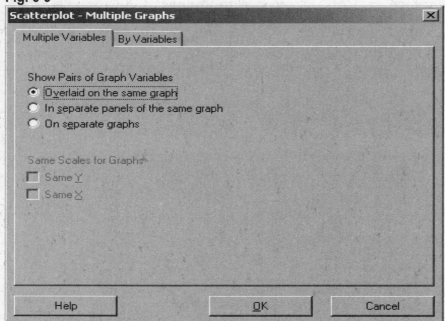

To graph the two curves on one page, click on the **Multiple Graphs** button. Select **Overlaid on the same graph.** Click on OK. (Fig. 6-9)

Fig. 6-9

Click on **OK** again and you should see the graphs (Fig. 6-10). Notice that they look identical, except that one is shifted over. This is because the two distributions have different means, but the same standard deviations. In the assignment below, you will explore what happens when the means are the same, but the standard deviations are different.

• •

Fig. 6-10

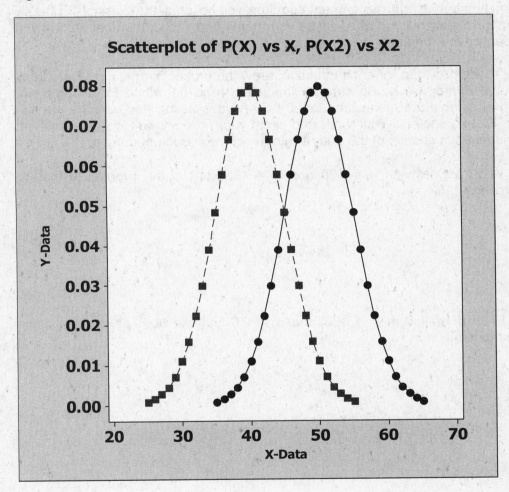

In the above figure (Fig. 6-10), identify which curve has a mean of 50 and which has a mean of 40.

Assignment

Please answer all questions in the space provided. When you have completed this assignment, tear the pages along the perforation. Include with this assignment all computer work that is required to answer the questions. Each graph must be labeled with a title, axis labels, and a footnote with your name and section number. If the assignment requires you to print the Session Window, click in the Session Window and type your name and section number so that you can identify your printout.

In the space provided for each question, draw the proper normal curve and label the curve appropriately. Be sure to shade the area described in the problem, identify and label the mean, and label the X-values associated with the shaded areas. Please show all your work and circle your final answer to each problem. Also, label each section of the output with the correct problem number.

1. If W is normal with $\mu = 100$ and $\sigma = 10$, what is the probability that W exceeds 115?

2. If W is normal with $\mu = 100$ and $\sigma = 10$, find the 90th percentile of this distribution.

3. If Y is normal with $\mu = 200$ and $\sigma = 10$, what is the probability that Y will be between 188 and 206?

4. If X is normal with μ = 8.48 and σ = 1.60, find the probability that X exceeds 6.96?

5. If X is normal with μ = 8.48 and σ = 1.60, what are the two values of X which include the central 80% of the probability?

6. If Z is standard normal, above what value of z is 1% of the probability? (Recall that μ = 0 and σ =1 for the standard normal).

7. If Y is normal with μ = 200 and σ = 11, between what two values of Y is the central 50% of the probability?

8. If SAT scores are normal with μ = 500 and σ = 50, what is the probability that a randomly selected person will have an SAT score higher than 680?

9. The MATH SAT Scores for all students who applied to the School of Engineering are normally distributed with $\mu = 629$ and $\sigma = 60$. The School of Engineering has decided to accept those students whose scores fall within the top 15%. What is the minimum score an applicant must have in order to be accepted into the Engineering School?

10. The average length of time required for students to complete a test in an Introductory Statistics course is found to be 50 minutes with a standard deviation of 12 minutes. If students are allowed 80 minutes to complete the test, approximately what percentage of the students will have sufficient time to complete the test? (Assume that the time required to complete the test follows a normal distribution.)

11. The daily sales at the campus bookstore throughout the school year have a probability distribution that is approximately normal with $\mu = \$1530$ and $\sigma = \$120$. The bookstore must have at least $1200 in sales per day to break even. What is the probability that on a given day the bookstore will not break even?

12. Use a graph to see the effect of changing the standard deviation of a normal distribution. Let μ = 100 for both distributions, but let σ = 10 for one and σ = 20 for the other distribution. Recall, that for each distribution the first X value should be 3σ below the mean of 100, and the last X value should be 3σ above the mean of 100. For both distributions, when you instruct MINITAB to create the X values for you, this time set the data **IN STEPS OF** 2. Graph both distributions on the same page.

   a. Explain what changing the standard deviation does to the distribution.

Chapter 7

The Central Limit Theorem and
the Sampling Distribution
of the Sample Mean

I N CHAPTER 6, we studied the normal probability distribution for a random variable, X. Based on this distribution, we can calculate probabilities for specific values of the random variable. For example, it is known that IQs are normally distributed with $\mu = 100$ and $\sigma = 15$. Suppose we want to calculate the probability that a randomly selected individual has an IQ greater than 130. That is, we wish to calculate P(X>130). This is easily done using MINITAB's normal probability distribution.

In this chapter, rather than looking at one person's IQ, we will consider the _average_ IQ for a sample of n individuals. Suppose we want to calculate P($\bar{x}$ > 130) for a sample of n = 35 individuals. This is an entirely different question from the one above because now we are asking to calculate the probability that the _average_ IQ for the group is greater than 130. What we are now asking is a probability question about $\bar{x}$, instead of X, so we need to study the behavior of $\bar{x}$. Since $\bar{x}$ is calculated from a **sample** of x's, the probability distribution of $\bar{x}$ is called a **Sampling Distribution**.

The Central Limit Theorem
....

You will discover in this lesson that the mean of the sampling distribution of $\bar{x}$, ($\mu_{\bar{x}}$), is equal to the mean of the original population (μ). The standard deviation of the sampling distribution of $\bar{x}$, ($\sigma_{\bar{x}}$), is approximately equal to the population standard deviation divided by the square root of n, ($\sigma / \sqrt{n}$). For "large" samples (n > 30), the sampling distribution of $\bar{x}$ is approximately normally distributed, regardless of the shape of the underlying population. This is the Central Limit Theorem, which you have probably studied in class by now.

In order to study the behavior of $\bar{x}$, we will create several sampling distributions in the following way:

1. Start with a population of x's.

2. From that population take a random sample of size n.

3. Calculate the mean, $\bar{x}$, of that sample.

4. Repeat this process (that is, take another random sample of size n and calculate the mean of this sample).

5. Repeat this process indefinitely and you would generate a population of means ($\bar{x}$'s). This is called the Sampling Distribution of the Sample Mean. (Note: in this lab you will create a "pseudo-population" by repeating the process a fixed number of times, rather than an indefinite number of times.)

101

The questions that we want to answer are the following:

a. How does the mean of the sampling distribution compare to the mean of the original population?

b. How does the standard deviation of the sampling distribution compare to the standard deviation of the original population?

c. How does the shape of the sampling distribution compare to the shape of the original population?

Applications of the Central Limit Theorem

Let's return to the example concerning the average IQ of a sample of 35 individuals. We know that IQs are normally distributed with mean =100 and standard deviation =15. The Central Limit Theorem tells us that for n=35 the Sampling Distribution of $\bar{x}$ is normally distributed with $\mu_{\bar{x}} = 100$ and $\sigma_{\bar{x}} = \sigma/\sqrt{n}$ = $15/\sqrt{35}$ = 2.54. Now suppose we are interested in calculating the probability that the average IQ for our group is greater than 105.

We can use MINITAB to calculate $P(\bar{x} > 105)$. To do this, we will use the same procedure that we used in Chapter 6 for Normal Probability Problems. However, since we are asking a probability question about $\bar{x}$, we must use the standard deviation of the sampling distribution of $\bar{x}$. This can be pre-calculated using either your hand calculator or MINITAB's calculator.

Now, let's calculate $P(\bar{x} > 105)$ for our sample of n=35 using MINITAB. To do this, click on:

CALC → PROBABILITY DISTRIBUTIONS → NORMAL

In the next window, select **CUMULATIVE PROBABILITY**. In this example, the **mean** is 100 and the **standard deviation** is 2.54 (which is $15/\sqrt{35}$). Next select **INPUT CONSTANT** and enter the value 105. Click on **OK** and the result that appears in the Session Window is $P(\bar{x} \leq 105)$ which is .9755. Since we are interested in $P(\bar{x} > 105)$, we must subtract .9755 from 1.

Assignment

••

Please answer all questions in the space provided. When you have completed this assignment, tear the pages along the perforation. Include with this assignment all computer work that is required to answer the questions. Each graph must be labeled with a title, axis labels, and a footnote with your name and section number. If the assignment requires you to print the Session Window, click in the Session Window and type your name and section number so you can identify your printout.

In this assignment, in order to study the behavior of $\bar{x}$, you will be generating random samples. Because the samples are random, each individual's samples will be different.

1. Begin with a population that is NORMAL with a mean of 100 and a standard deviation of 10. Take 300 random samples of size n=2.

    To do this, click on: CALC → RANDOM DATA → NORMAL

    On the input screen that appears, **Generate** 300 **rows of data**, **store in** C1 and C2. Be sure to enter the **mean** = 100 and **standard deviation** = 10. After you click on **OK**, you should see data in the Data Window in C1 and C2. Each **row** represents a random sample of n=2 data points from the population.

    Now use ROW STATISTICS to calculate the mean for each sample of n=2.

    To do this, click on: CALC → ROW STATISTICS.

    On the input screen that appears, select **MEAN**. Use C1-C2 as the **input variables** and **store result in** C3.

    Now look at the different columns. Name C3 so that when you graph the histograms, you will be able to identify the sampling distribution easily. To do this, click on the Data Window to move the cursor down to it. In the gray cell at the top of C3, type in "Nor(n=2)" to identify the distribution and sample size. Each entry in C3 should be the average of the values in C1 and C2. Use your calculator to verify this by choosing any row and averaging the values in C1 and C2 and confirm that this is the corresponding value in C3. Show your calculation below.

What you have created in C3 approximately represents a Sampling Distribution of $\bar{x}$. Find the mean and standard deviation of the Sampling Distribution. To do this, click on:

STAT → BASIC STATISTICS → DISPLAY DESCRIPTIVE STATISTICS

On the input screen that appears, select C3 for the **Variable.** The results will be in the Session Window. **(*Wait until after problem 5 to print the Session Window.*)**

a. How does the mean of C3 ($\mu_{\bar{x}}$) compare to the mean of the original population, μ? Recall that the mean of the original population is 100. (Note: $\mu_{\bar{x}}$ should be approximately equal to μ).

   $\mu_{\bar{x}} =$ _____

Are the two values close? _____ If so, the results of your simulation of a sampling distribution confirm that: $\mu_{\bar{x}}$ should be approximately equal to μ.

b. How does $\sigma_{\bar{x}}$, the standard deviation of C3, compare to the standard deviation of the original population, σ? (Note: $\sigma_{\bar{x}}$ should be approx. equal to $\sigma/\sqrt{n}$). For this example, n = 2 and σ = 10.

   Using your calculator, calculate $\sigma/\sqrt{n}$. _____

   Compare your calculation to the standard deviation of C3. _____

   Are the two numbers close? _____ If so, the results of your simulation of a sampling distribution confirm that $\sigma_{\bar{x}}$ should be approx. equal to $\sigma/\sqrt{n}$.

c. Now compare the shape of a set of data from the original population, C1, with the shape of the sampling distribution, C3. To do this, click on: GRAPH → HISTOGRAM. Click on the SIMPLE histogram icon. Select both C1 and C3 for the GRAPH VARIABLES. If you then click on the button labeled MULTIPLE GRAPHS, you can select **SAME Y** and also **SAME X, including bins** by clicking on the check boxes. Now both histograms will have the same scale. Put a title on the graphs. The title should identify the distribution (Normal) and the sample size (n=2). ***Do Not** use Axis Labels here. Let MINITAB use the column name so that you can tell which column of data the histogram is displaying.* Print the two histograms. In the space below write a summary of the similarities and differences between the shapes of the two columns. Be specific.

Comment on which histograms look normal. Compare the centers and spreads of the two graphs.

2. Next begin with a population that is not normal. We will use a UNIFORM distribution with endpoints 70 and 130. A UNIFORM distribution has a flat shape with data that is evenly distributed. It looks like a rectangle.   (Fig. 7-1)

• •

Fig. 7-1

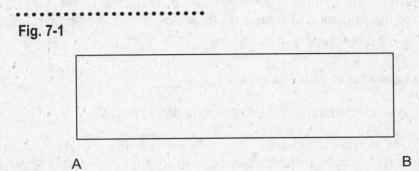

A   B

The values of A and B represent the endpoints of the distribution. In our example, A will be 70 and B will be 130.

To start with a clear Data Window, highlight and delete all data cells. This should give you a blank Data Window, but the Session Window should still have the **Descriptive Statistics** from the last example. Take 300 random samples of size n=2 from a UNIFORM distribution on the interval 70 to 130. Use the commands described above in problem 1, except this time select **UNIFORM** distribution with **lower endpoint** 70 and **upper endpoint** 130. Use **ROW STATISTICS** to calculate the mean for each sample of n=2 and **store results in** C3. Name C3 appropriately, i.e. "Uni(n=2)".

Each entry in C3 should be the average of the values in C1 and C2. Verify this by choosing any row and averaging the values in C1 and C2 and confirm that this is the corresponding value in C3. Show this work below.

What you have created in C3 is a representation of the Sampling Distribution of $\bar{x}$.

a. Use **DISPLAY DESCRIPTIVE STATISTICS** for C3 to find the mean and standard deviation of the values in C3.

How does the mean of C3 compare to the mean of the original population? (The mean of the original population is 100).

$\mu_{\bar{x}} = \underline{\hspace{2cm}}$

Are the two values close? $\underline{\hspace{2cm}}$ If so, the results of your simulation of a sampling distribution confirm that $\mu_{\bar{x}}$ should be approximately equal to μ.

b. How does $\sigma_{\bar{x}}$, the standard deviation of C3, compare to the standard deviation of the original population, σ? (Note: $\sigma_{\bar{x}}$ should be approx. equal to $\sigma/\sqrt{n}$). For this example, n = 2 and σ = 17.3.

    Using your calculator, calculate $\sigma/\sqrt{n}$. $\underline{\hspace{2.5cm}}$

    Compare your calculation to the standard deviation of C3. $\underline{\hspace{2.5cm}}$

    Are the two numbers close? $\underline{\hspace{2cm}}$ If so, the results of your simulation of a sampling distribution confirm that $\sigma_{\bar{x}}$ should be approx. equal to $\sigma/\sqrt{n}$.

c. Now compare the shape of data from the original population in C1 with the shape of the sampling distribution in C3. To do this, use the same procedure for making histograms as was described above in problem 1. Use C1 and C3 for the histrograms. Be sure to title the histograms with the distribution and sample size. Print the two histograms. In the space below write a summary of the similarities and differences between the shapes of the two columns. Be specific. Be sure to comment on shape, center, and variation for each histogram.

3. Continue this example with the Uniform distribution, but increase the sample size from n=2 to n=30. Again, start with a clear worksheet. This time you need to **generate** 300 **rows of data** and **store in** C1-C30. Now each row represents a sample of n=30 data points from the population. Use **ROW STATISTICS** to calculate the **mean** for each sample of n=30. The **input variables** should be C1-C30, and you can **store result in** C31. Name C31 "Uni(n=30)". Each entry in C31 should be the average of the values in C1

through C30. What you have created in C31 is a representation of the Sampling Distribution of $\bar{x}$.

a. Use the **DISPLAY DESCRIPTIVE STATISTICS** on C31 to find the mean and standard deviation of the values in C31.

How does the mean of C31 compare to the mean of the original population? (The mean of original population is 100).

$\mu_{\bar{x}}$ = _____

Are the two values close? _____ If so, the results of your simulation of a sampling distribution confirm that $\mu_{\bar{x}}$ should be approximately equal to μ.

b. How does $\sigma_{\bar{x}}$, the standard deviation of C31, compare to the standard deviation of the original population, σ? (Note: $\sigma_{\bar{x}}$ should be approx. equal to $\sigma / \sqrt{n}$). For this example, n = 30 and σ = 17.3.

Using your calculator, calculate $\sigma / \sqrt{n}$. _____

Compare your calculation to the standard deviation of C31. _____

Are the two numbers close? _____ If so, the results of your simulation of a sampling distribution confirm that $\sigma_{\bar{x}}$ should be approx. equal to $\sigma / \sqrt{n}$.

c. Now compare the shape of data from the original population with the shape of the sampling distribution. Use C1 and C31 for the histograms. Use the same procedure as described above to get the same scale for both graphs. Be sure to change the title of your graphs to indicate that n=30. Print the histograms. In the space below write a summary of the similarities and differences between the shapes of the two columns. Be specific.

4. The daily sales at the campus bookstore throughout the school year have a probability distribution that is approximately normal with mean = $1530 and standard deviation = $120. The bookstore must have a monthly **average** of at least $1500 to break even. Assuming a month has 30 days, what is the probability that, for a given month, the bookstore breaks even?

$\mu_{\bar{x}} =$ _____

$\sigma_{\bar{x}} =$ _____

$P(\bar{x} \leq 1500) =$ _____

$P(\bar{x} > 1500) =$ _____

So the probability that the bookstore breaks even in a given month is _____.

5. On a particular stretch of highway, the State Police know that the average speed is 62 mph with a standard deviation of 5 mph. On a busy holiday weekend, the police are concerned that people travel too fast. So they randomly monitor speeds of a sample of 50 cars and record an average speed of 66 mph. Find the probability of obtaining a sample average speed of 66 mph or more if, in fact, the true average speed on that holiday weekend is still 62 mph?

$\mu_{\bar{x}}$ = _____

$\sigma_{\bar{x}}$ = _____

$P(\bar{x} \leq 66)$ = _____

$P(\bar{x} > 66)$ = _____

The probability that the average speed of the sample is greater than 66 mph is _____.

Based on this probability, are the police justified in their concern?
Explain your answer.

Chapter 8

Confidence Interval Estimation

ONE OF THE very important statistical inference problems is estimation. Estimation is concerned with finding the value of a population parameter (for example, μ, the population mean), without actually obtaining the data from the entire population. Instead of working with an entire population you can simply take a random sample from the population and use the sample information to provide an estimate of the population parameter.

There are two types of estimation methods: point estimation and interval estimation. For example, you can calculate the mean of a sample and use this to estimate the mean of the population from which the sample was taken. In this case, the sample mean, $\overline{x}$, is a *point estimate* of the population mean, μ. Alternatively, you can use the sample mean as a starting point and add a margin of error, creating an *interval estimate* of μ.

Any sample is usually only a small part of the population, so it is very unlikely that the sample mean will be *exactly* equal to the population mean, but we hope it will be close. Since μ is unknown, there is no way to know how close $\overline{x}$, the point estimate, is to μ. Because of this uncertainty, point estimates are used less frequently than interval estimates.

An interval estimate uses a range of values to estimate μ. To create the interval, start with the sample mean, $\overline{x}$, since it is our "best guess" of the value of μ. Now add and subtract a margin of error. The margin of error depends upon the standard deviation of the sampling distribution of $\overline{x}$ and the "confidence coefficient".

Before we look at any intervals, let's discuss the confidence coefficient. It measures the confidence we have in the process we are using to construct the interval, which is called a *confidence interval*. For example, if you choose a 95% confidence coefficient and you construct hundreds of confidence intervals, then approximately 95% of these intervals will include μ, the true population mean and 5% of them will fail to include μ. These intervals that fail to include μ are usually the result of obtaining a random sample in which $\overline{x}$ is very different from μ. Of course, since μ is unknown, you cannot determine which of the intervals DO contain μ and which intervals DO NOT contain μ. However, you "have confidence" that the process you used will result in an interval that contains μ, the true mean of the populations, 95% of the time.

Confidence Interval Formulas:

•••

There are two basic confidence interval formulas for μ, the Z-Interval and the t-Interval.

The Z - confidence interval for μ is:

$$\bar{x} \pm z^* \sigma / \sqrt{n}$$

This formula is used when the population is normally distributed and σ is known. The z value in the formula comes from the standard normal table and is based on the confidence coefficient (typically 90%, 95%, 99%).

The t- confidence interval for μ is:

$$\bar{x} \pm t^* s / \sqrt{n}$$

This formula is used when the population is normally distributed and σ is unknown. The t value in the formula comes from the t-table and is based on the confidence coefficient.

If you look at the two formulas, you will notice that they are very similar. Both formulas start with $\bar{x}$, a point estimate of μ, and add and subtract a margin of error. The margin of error is composed of a table value (Z or t), a standard deviation (σ or s), and a sample size. Both formulas apply to normally distributed data. In fact, that restriction can be relaxed as n (the sample size) increases. It is only when n is small (approximately 20 or less) that normality is critical. Regardless of sample size, it is always a good idea to plot the data and look for outliers (unusual data points) and for skewness in the data. But, these concerns are more serious in small samples.

In practice, σ, the population standard deviation, is rarely known, so the Z-interval is not used very often. Note: Some textbooks recommend the use of the Z-interval for large samples (n > 30), even when σ is unknown. In these cases, s, the sample standard deviation, is a good approximation for σ and is used in place of σ in the formula. For large samples, the Z-interval and t-interval will yield almost identical results.

Example 1:

In this example, you will study the process of constructing confidence intervals. You will begin with a normally distributed population with a known mean equal to 69 and a known standard deviation equal to 3. From this population, select 50 random samples of size n=30. To do this, click on:

CALC → RANDOM DATA → NORMAL

In the screen that appears, you want to:

Generate: 30 rows (since n=30)
Store in: C1 – C50 (since we want 50 samples)
Mean: 69
Standard Deviation: 3

Each of the 50 columns is a random sample of size n=30 from the normal population with μ=69 and σ=3. Now use the 50 columns of data to construct 50 different 95% confidence intervals for μ. Each confidence interval is an interval estimate of μ. In this example, we already know that μ is equal to 69, so we can actually see how well the confidence intervals do at estimating μ. Since σ is known, use the 1-Sample z.

To construct the intervals, click on:

STAT → BASIC STATISTICS → 1-SAMPLE-Z

In the screen that appears, you will use each of the 50 columns to construct 50 different confidence intervals. Under **Samples in columns:** type in C1-C50. Enter the population standard deviation, 3. Click on **Options** and enter 95 for the **Confidence Interval.** The confidence intervals will appear in the Session Window. **Maximize** the Session Window to easily view the confidence intervals. (Fig. 8-1).

Note: Your intervals will be different since this is RANDOM data.

●●●●●●●●●●●●●●●●●●●●●●●●

Fig. 8-1

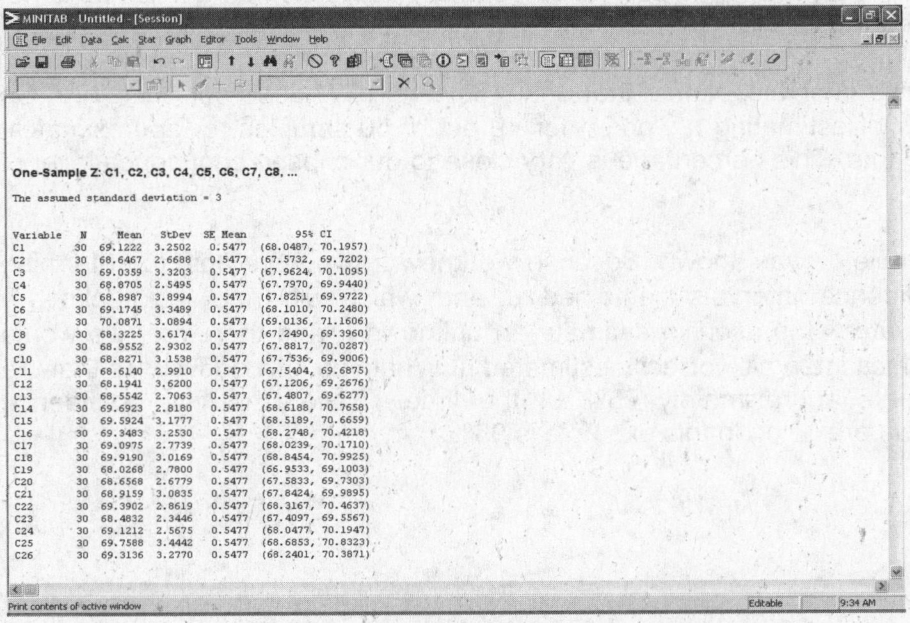

One-Sample Z: C1, C2, C3, C4, C5, C6, C7, C8, ...

The assumed standard deviation = 3

Variable	N	Mean	StDev	SE Mean	95% CI
C1	30	69.1222	3.2502	0.5477	(68.0487, 70.1957)
C2	30	68.6467	2.6688	0.5477	(67.5732, 69.7202)
C3	30	69.0359	3.3203	0.5477	(67.9624, 70.1095)
C4	30	68.8705	2.5495	0.5477	(67.7970, 69.9440)
C5	30	68.8987	3.8994	0.5477	(67.8251, 69.9722)
C6	30	69.1745	3.3489	0.5477	(68.1010, 70.2480)
C7	30	70.0871	3.0894	0.5477	(69.0136, 71.1606)
C8	30	68.3225	3.6174	0.5477	(67.2490, 69.3960)
C9	30	68.9552	2.9302	0.5477	(67.8817, 70.0287)
C10	30	68.8271	3.1538	0.5477	(67.7536, 69.9006)
C11	30	68.6140	2.9910	0.5477	(67.5404, 69.6875)
C12	30	68.1941	3.6200	0.5477	(67.1206, 69.2676)
C13	30	68.5542	2.7063	0.5477	(67.4807, 69.6277)
C14	30	69.6923	2.8180	0.5477	(68.6188, 70.7658)
C15	30	69.5924	3.1777	0.5477	(68.5189, 70.6659)
C16	30	69.3483	3.2530	0.5477	(68.2748, 70.4218)
C17	30	69.0975	2.7739	0.5477	(68.0239, 70.1710)
C18	30	69.9190	3.0169	0.5477	(68.8454, 70.9925)
C19	30	68.0268	2.7800	0.5477	(66.9533, 69.1003)
C20	30	68.6568	2.6779	0.5477	(67.5833, 69.7303)
C21	30	68.9159	3.0835	0.5477	(67.8424, 69.9895)
C22	30	69.3902	2.8619	0.5477	(68.3167, 70.4637)
C23	30	68.4832	2.3446	0.5477	(67.4097, 69.5567)
C24	30	69.1212	2.5675	0.5477	(68.0477, 70.1947)
C25	30	69.7588	3.4442	0.5477	(68.6853, 70.8323)
C26	30	69.3136	3.2770	0.5477	(68.2401, 70.3871)

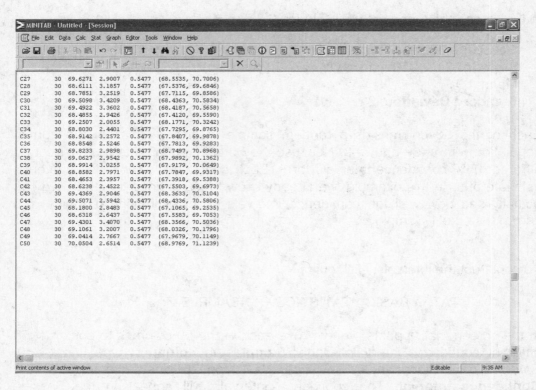

Each row contains information about one of your samples of data. For example, the first row shows N, MEAN, STDEV, SE MEAN and 95% CI for the first set of 30 data points that you randomly generated in C1. The 95% confidence interval for the first sample is (68.0487, 70.1957). Recall that μ is 69 in this population,. So this particular confidence interval DID accurately estimate μ since 69 lies between the lower limit of the confidence interval (68.0487) and the upper limit (70.1957). Now notice the confidence interval that was created from the data in C7: (69.0136, 71.1606). This interval failed to correctly estimate μ since 69 is not contained in the interval.

Look at all 50 intervals. Notice that only 1 interval (C7) does not contain μ. So this process of estimating μ worked for 49 out of 50 samples, or approximately 98% of the time. This percentage is very close to our chosen confidence level of 95%.

In this example, μ was known. Because we knew μ, we were able to determine which confidence intervals contained μ and which did not. In practice, a confidence interval is used to estimate an unknown μ and therefore, we would not know which intervals correctly estimated μ. What you saw above was that the process works approximately 95% of the time. (Recall that the confidence coefficient we are using in this example is 95%.)

Example 2:

For this example, you will enter the data directly into C1 in the Data Window. Start by clearing the current worksheet.

Here is a random sample of final exam scores for 20 randomly selected students in a large Introductory Statistics class.

   88 67 73 65 89 77 81 94 99 54 65 56 79 88 72 64 55 69 71 55

You are interested in constructing a confidence interval for μ, the average exam grade for all students in the course.

Since this is a small dataset it is critical that the assumption of normality is satisfied. So we will begin with a graph that will look for normality (or lack of normality).

Click on: GRAPH → PROBABILITY PLOTS and select Single. On the screen that appears, select C1 as your **Graph Variable.** Click on **OK**, and a Normal Probability Plot of the data will appear. If the data points   are fairly linear, then the data is approximately normal. Note: We will look at this graph and its output in more detail when we study Hypothesis Testing in the next chapter. (Fig. 8-2)

Fig. 8-2

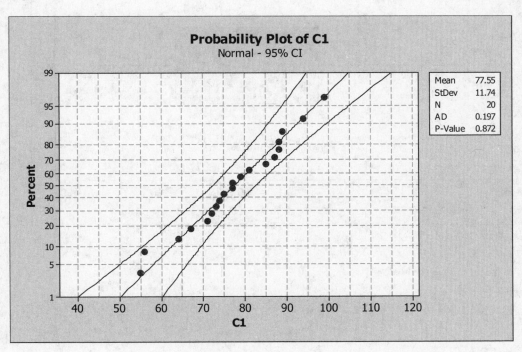

The graph shows the data points with a line drawn through the points and with confidence bands on either side of the line. The graph shows that there is some scatter of the points around the line but that the data generally falls in a linear pattern.

Now, you are ready to proceed with the t-interval.

Click on: STAT → BASIC STATISTICS → 1-SAMPLE t

Click on: **Graphs** and select Histogram and Boxplot.

Click on: **Options** and set the Confidence level to 95.

The graphs and the Confidence interval will be displayed. (Fig. 8-3).

● ●
Fig. 8-3

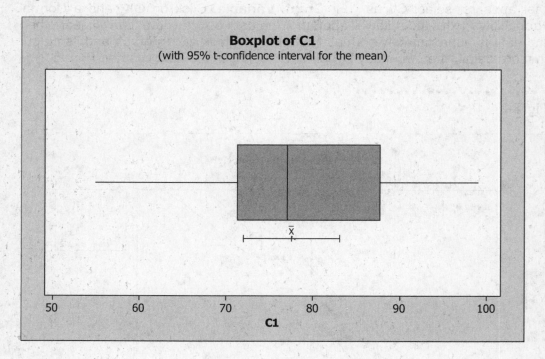

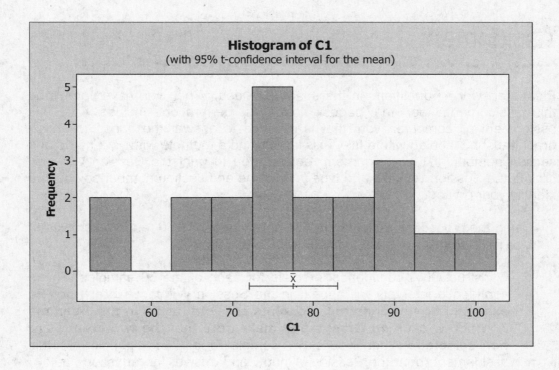

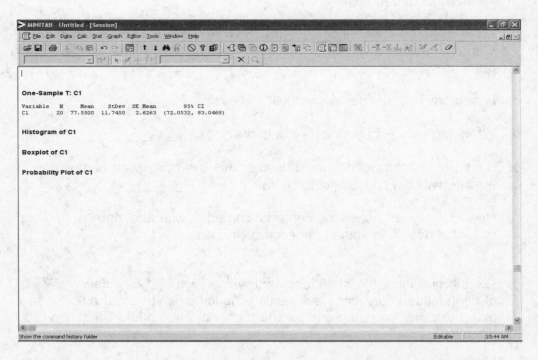

The graphs give us a "snapshot" of the data. The boxplot shows that there is no problem with outliers or with skewness in the data. The histogram also shows that the data is fairly symmetric. The Session Window contains descriptive statistics for the sample and a 95% Confidence Interval for μ. The Confidence Interval states that the average score on the exam was between 72.05 and 83.05.

Assignment

....

Please answer all questions in the space provided. When you have completed this assignment, tear the pages along the perforation. Include with this assignment all computer work that is required to answer the questions. Each graph must be labeled with a title, axis labels, and a footnote with your name and section number. If the assignment requires you to print the Session Window, click in the Session Window and type your name and section number so you can identify your printout.

1. Using the procedure explained in Example 1 generate 50 random samples of size n=30 from a normal population with μ=69 and σ=3.

   a. Construct 90% confidence intervals for each of the 50 samples. These confidence intervals will appear in the Session Window. **Note: For this example, do not construct Boxplots or Histograms. In the 1-sample Z Window, click on Graphs and make sure that the two graphs are not selected.** When you have completed all the examples in this assignment, print the Session Window and answer the questions below. Now proceed to problem #2.

   b. Look at the 50 confidence intervals. How many of your intervals failed to correctly estimate μ? _____ (Highlight these intervals on your printout.)

   c. How many of your intervals actually did contain μ? _____

   d. What percentage of your intervals contained μ? _____

   e. Based on the confidence level used in this example, what percentage of the intervals did you expect to contain μ? _____

   f. How does your actual percentage compare with the percentage you expected based on your confidence coefficient?

   g. For the first five 95% confidence intervals in Fig. 8-1 calculate the width of confidence intervals by subtracting the lower limit from the upper limit and rounding your answer to the nearest hundredth. What did you discover?

h. For the first five 90% confidence intervals that you created in your Session Window calculate the width of the intervals and round your answer to the nearest hundredth. What did you discover?

i. How does the width of the 95% confidence intervals compare to the width of the 90% confidence intervals?

2. Do an analysis of the confidence interval process for the situation where σ is unknown. Open the worksheet CONFINT1.MTW. This file contains 50 random samples of size n=25 from a normal population with μ=69.

a. Construct 90% confidence intervals for each of the 50 samples, C1-C50. Since σ is unknown, you will use the **1-Sample-t** to create the confidence intervals.

Click on: STAT → BASIC STATISTICS → 1-SAMPLE-t

Fill in the appropriate information in the input windows. **Note: For this example, do not construct Boxplots or Histograms. Click on Graphs and make sure that the two graphs are not selected.**

b. Answer the following questions after you print your Session Window. Proceed to problem #3.

c. Look at the 50 confidence intervals. How many of your intervals failed to correctly estimate μ? _____ (Highlight these intervals on your printout.)

d. How many of your intervals actually did contain μ? _____

e. What percentage of your intervals contained μ? _____

f. Based on the confidence level used in this example, what percentage of the intervals did you expect to contain μ? _____

g. How does your actual percentage compare with the percentage you expected based on your confidence coefficient?

h. For the first five 90% confidence intervals that you created in your Session Window calculate the width of the intervals and round your answer to the nearest hundredth. What did you discover?

i. Compare the 90% t-intervals to the 90% Z-intervals calculated in problem 1a.

j. Suppose you created 99% t-intervals instead of 90% t-intervals. What differences would you expect?

3. For this example, you will enter the data directly into the Data Window. Start by clearing the current worksheet.

Here is a random sample of resting heart rates for 20 male athletes between the ages of 18 and 25:

58 67 63 65 59 57 51 64 59 54 65 56 59 58 62 64 55 59 61 55

You are interested in constructing a confidence interval for μ, the average heart rate of all male athletes in this age group.

Since this is a small dataset it is critical that the assumption of normality is satisfied. So begin with a graph that will look for normality (or lack of normality).

a. Construct a 99% confidence interval for μ, the average heart rate of all male athletes in this age group. Include a Histogram and Boxplot of the data.

b. What do the graphs (probability plot, Histogram and Boxplot) tell you about the dataset?

c. Using the confidence interval, make a statement about μ, the average resting heart rate of male athletes.

4. Suppose you are interested in estimating the average salary for Biostatisticians in Connecticut. You obtain a random sample of 25 biostatisticians hired during the last five years. The sample data appeared to be approximately normally distributed with no outliers. The average salary for the sample is $45,000 and the standard deviation is $3150. Construct a 95% confidence interval for μ the true average salary for newly hired biostatisticians in Connecticut.

Note: In this example, you have the *summarized data*, rather than the *raw data*.

Click on: STAT → BASIC STATISTICS → 1-SAMPLE-t

On the input screen, select **Summarized Data** and enter the sample size, the sample mean and the sample standard deviation.

Note: Be sure to print your Session Window now.

Chapter 9

Hypothesis Testing
(One Sample Problem)

A TEST OF HYPOTHESIS is a statistical technique for making decisions about a population parameter. Hypothesis testing is used in scientific research and in business and financial decision-making. As the name suggests, a test of hypothesis begins with a new theory, or hypothesis, that differs from the current theory. The researcher must gather evidence to support the new idea. The new theory is called the **alternative hypothesis** (H_A) and the current theory is called the **null hypothesis** (H_0). In a test of hypothesis, it is assumed that the null hypothesis is true, until there is overwhelming evidence to the contrary. If the data provides such evidence, the researcher can conclude that the alternative hypothesis is true. Statistically, the new theory can then be accepted as true.

Any test of hypothesis starts with the identification of the null and alternative hypotheses. A sample of data is then collected, checked for errors, and analyzed to see if the data is reasonably consistent with the null hypothesis or if it contradicts the null. This is done by summarizing the information in the sample data and calculating a test statistic. The sample data contradict the null hypothesis when the test statistic differs significantly from what would be expected if the null hypothesis were true.

For example, suppose the current treatment for high blood pressure provides a mean reduction of 20 points. A pharmaceutical company is testing a new drug which they believe will be more effective in reducing blood pressure. Their research hypothesis (H_A) is that the mean blood pressure drop under the new treatment is more than 20 points. The null hypothesis (H_0) is that the mean drop in blood pressure is 20 points. The company expects that the data will contradict the null hypothesis and thus, supply evidence that their new drug more effectively lowers high blood pressure.

Since hypothesis testing, like interval estimation, uses a sample from the population, there is a possibility of making an incorrect decision and rejecting the null hypothesis when, in fact, it is true. A researcher incorporates this possibility into her hypothesis test by setting the significance level for the test. The significance level (α-level) measures the likelihood of this possibility. Typical α-levels are .10, .05, and .01. So if $\alpha = .05$, the probability of incorrectly rejecting the null hypothesis is .05.

Hypothesis Testing for a Mean

....

The procedure for the hypothesis test is to compare the sample mean to the population mean that is specified in the null hypothesis. We ASSUME that the null hypothesis is true, and would like to know if the sample mean is consistent with this assumption. The problem is that we need an objective way to decide if the sample data contradicts or agrees with the null hypothesis. Is the sample mean significantly different from the population mean, or is it only slightly different? We have already learned that a Z-score measures distance away from the mean. We will use it now in hypothesis testing, and call it a TEST STATISTIC. Recall that a Z-score is calculated by subtracting a mean and dividing by a standard deviation. Here we will be standardizing $\bar{x}$, our sample mean.

According to the Central Limit Theorem, $\mu_{\bar{x}} = \mu$ (the population mean which is specified in the null hypothesis) and $\sigma_{\bar{x}} = \sigma / \sqrt{n}$. These are the values to use in the calculation of the Z-score. Since we are standardizing $\bar{x}$, we subtract its mean (μ) and divide by its standard deviation ($\sigma / \sqrt{n}$). This TEST STATISTIC now measures how far the sample mean, $\bar{x}$, is from the hypothesized value for μ in the null hypothesis. It is written:

$$Z = \frac{\bar{x} - \hat{\imath}}{\acute{o} / \sqrt{n}}$$

Since our test statistic is a Z-score, we can calculate its location on a standard normal curve. The farther the Z-score is from the center of the normal curve, the more unlikely it is, if the null hypothesis is true. To measure how unlikely the Z-score is, we calculate the tail area in the standard normal curve beyond this Z-score. This area is called the "P-value." Compare the P-value to the significance level for the test (σ-level). If the P-value is less than the σ-level, we will reject the null hypothesis in favor of the alternative hypothesis.

If σ, the population standard deviation is unknown, then the calculation of the TEST STATISTIC changes to a t-value:

$$t = \frac{\bar{x} - \mu}{s / \sqrt{n}}$$

If you compare the t-calculation to the Z-calculation, you will notice that the formulas are quite similar. In the t-formula, the sample standard deviation, s, is used. In the Z-formula, the population standard deviation, σ, is used. In practice, σ, the population standard deviation, is rarely known. So, the Z formula is not used very often.

Note: Some textbooks recommend the use of the Z-formula for large samples (n>30) even when σ is unknown. In these cases, s, the sample standard deviation, is a good approximation for σ and is used in place of σ in the Z-formula.

Both formulas apply to normally distributed data. In fact, that restriction can be relaxed as n (the sample size) increases. It is only when n is small that normality is critical.

Hypothesis Testing for a Population Proportion

A test of hypothesis about a population proportion is done similarly to a test about a population mean. The null and alternative hypotheses are statements about the population proportion, instead of the population mean. Sample data is collected and analyzed to see if the sample proportion, $\hat{p}$, is very different from the population proportion, p_0, as stated in the null hypothesis. We will again use a Z-score for our test statistic, but it will look very different from the one used above. We have studied the sampling distribution of the sample proportion, $\hat{p}$, and know that $\mu_{\hat{p}} = p_0$ (the population proportion specified in the null hypothesis) and $\sigma_{\hat{p}} = \sqrt{p_0 q_0 / n}$. So these are the values we use to calculate the test statistic (Z-score). Since we are standardizing the sample proportion, we subtract its mean (p_0) and divide by its standard deviation ($\sqrt{p_0 q_0 / n}$). Thus, our test statistic is:

$$Z = (\hat{p} - p_0) / \sqrt{p_0 q_0 / n}$$

The P-value is calculated and is compared to the σ-level, just as it is in the hypothesis test for a mean.

**Note: All examples below use EXAMPLE9.MTW to demonstrate how to fill in the input screens

Tests for a Mean (Z-Test)

Example 1:

In this example, we will look at a hypothesis test for μ, in the case where σ, the population standard deviation, is a known value.

Open the worksheet Example9.MTW.

The data in C1, (Example1), is a random sample of the amount of money spent last semester on books and supplies for a statistics course at a local university. Use this data to test the claim that the average cost is more than \$100. That is, test H_0: $\mu = 100$ vs. H_A: $\mu > 100$ at $\alpha = .05$. Suppose that, based on data from the previous semester, we have estimated that σ, the population standard deviation, is \$15.00.

The first step should always be to check the data. Since this data set is large, (n=50), the normality requirement is not critical. It is sufficient to check for extreme skewness and for outliers. You can do this as part of the hypothesis test in MINITAB.

Click on: STAT $\rightarrow$ BASIC STATISTICS $\rightarrow$ 1-SAMPLE Z

In the screen that appears (Fig. 9-1), MINITAB is expecting the following:

> **Samples in columns:** the column with sample data
> **Standard deviation:** the value for σ
> **Test Mean:** the value of μ from the null hypothesis

. . . .
Fig. 9-1

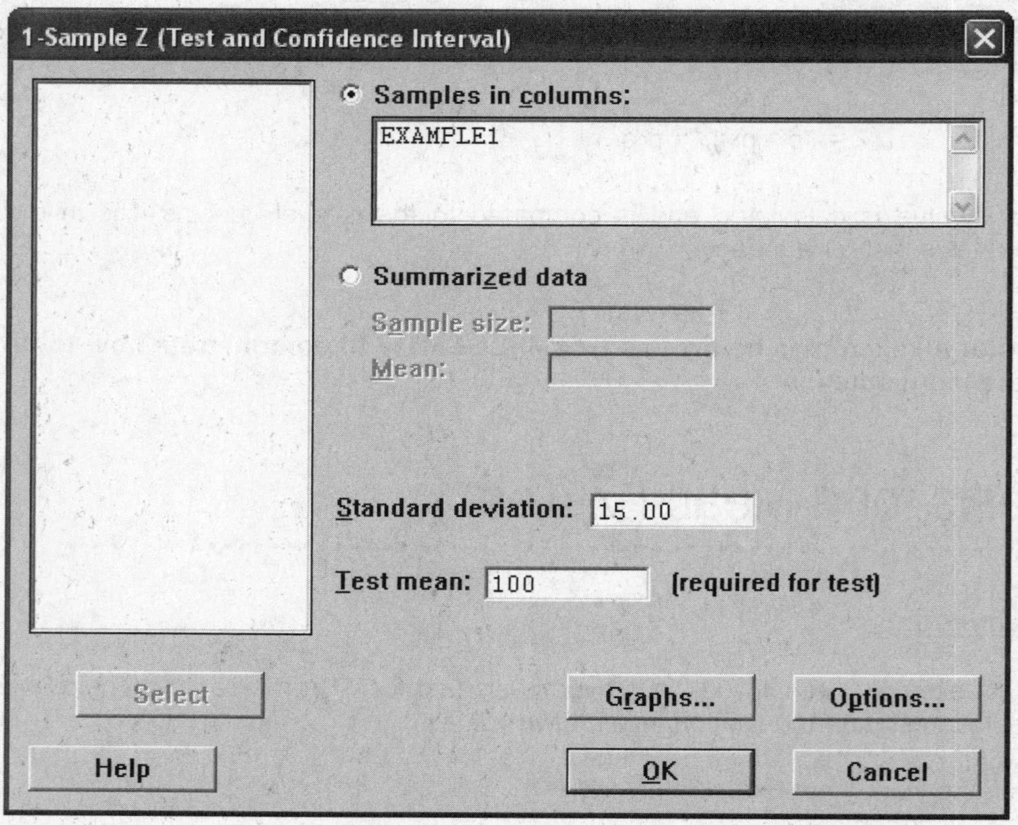

Click on: **Graphs** and select Histogram and Boxplot.

Click on: **Options** and set the **Alternative** to greater than. (Fig. 9-2)

Fig. 9-2

1-Sample Z - Options
Confidence level:
95.0
Alternative:
greater than
Help
OK
Cancel

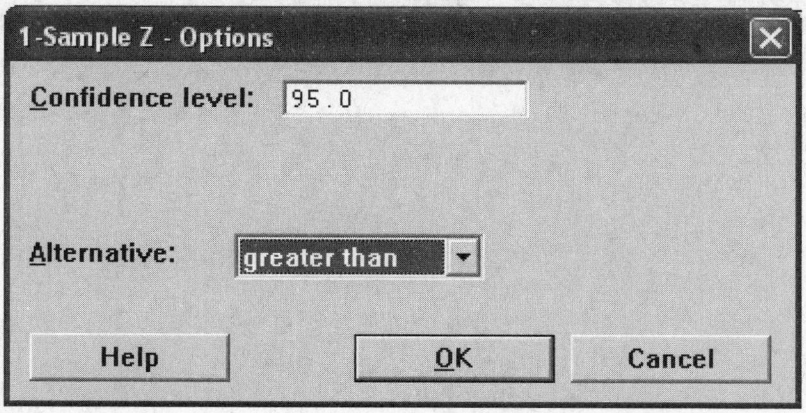

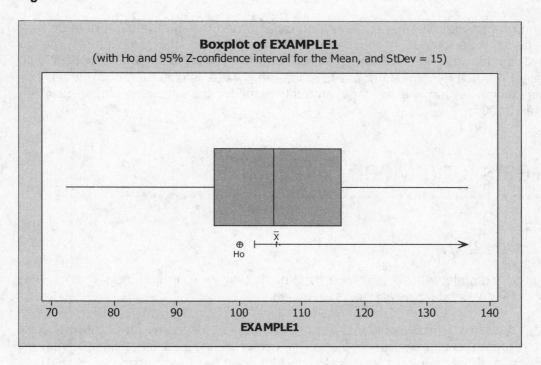

Click on Ok twice and the graphs and the hypothesis test will be displayed. (Fig. 9-3).

Fig. 9-3

Boxplot of EXAMPLE1
(with Ho and 95% Z-confidence interval for the Mean, and StDev = 15)
X̄
Ho
70
80
90
100
110
120
130
140
EXAMPLE1

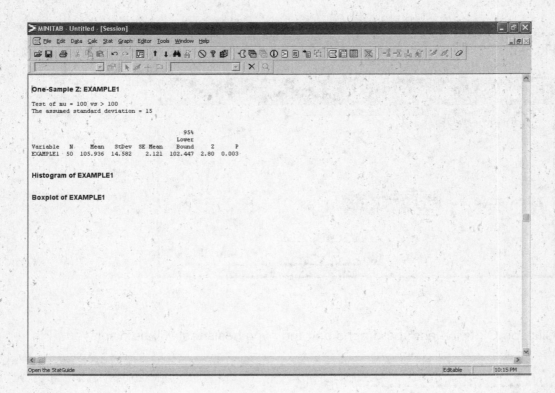

The graphs indicate that there are no outliers and that the data is not extremely skewed. The output in the Session Window shows the null and alternative hypotheses, the test statistic Z = 2.80, and the p-value P = .003. So we would reject the null hypothesis at α=.05 since the p-value is less than our α-level. Our conclusion is that the average amount spent for the statistics course is more than $100.

Tests for a Mean (T-Test)

Example 2:

In this example, we will look at a hypothesis test for μ, in the case where σ, the population standard deviation, is unknown.

The data in C2, (Example2), is a random sample of the amount of money spent at a local pizzeria by 20 couples. The owner of the pizzeria believes that, on average, most couples spend less than $30. Test her theory using H_0: μ = 30 vs. H_A: μ < 30 at α = .01.

Notice, from the Data Window, that n = 20 for this sample of data so it is critical that the assumption of normality is satisfied. So we will begin with a graph that will look for normality (or lack of normality).

Click on: GRAPH → PROBABILITY PLOTS and select Single. On the screen that appears, select C2 as your **Graph Variable.** Click on **OK**, and a Normal Probability Plot of the data will appear. If the data points are fairly linear, then the data is approximately normal. A P-value is printed at the right of the graph. This P-value is calculated for the test of hypothesis: H_0: Data is normally distributed vs. H_A: Data is not normally distributed. If the p-value is greater than .05, we DO NOT reject the null hypothesis and we conclude that the data is normally distributed. (In this example, you will find that the sample is approximately normal.) (Fig. 9-4)

. . . .
Fig. 9-4

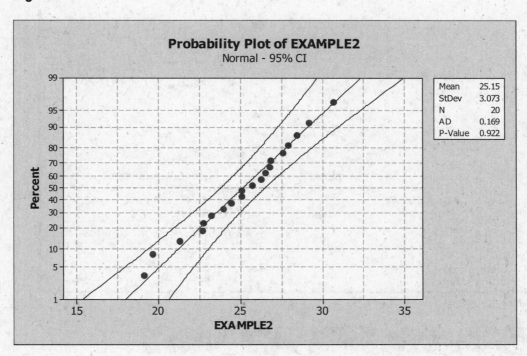

Now, you are ready to proceed with the t-test.

Click on: STAT → BASIC STATISTICS → 1-SAMPLE t

In the screen that appears (Fig. 9-5), MINITAB is expecting the following:

    Samples in columns: Example2
    Test Mean: 30

Click on: **Graphs** and select Histogram and Boxplot.

Click on: **Options** and select the appropriate Alternative hypothesis. (Fig. 9-5)

Fig. 9-5

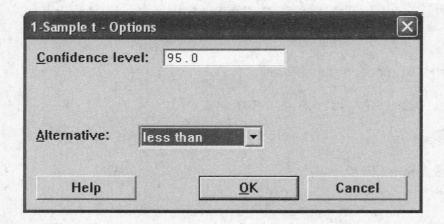

Click on **OK** twice and the graphs and test results will be displayed.

(Fig. 9-6)

Fig. 9-6

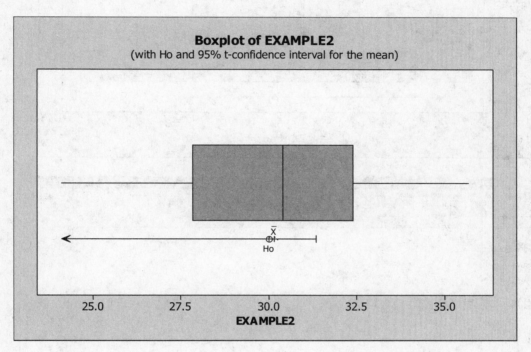

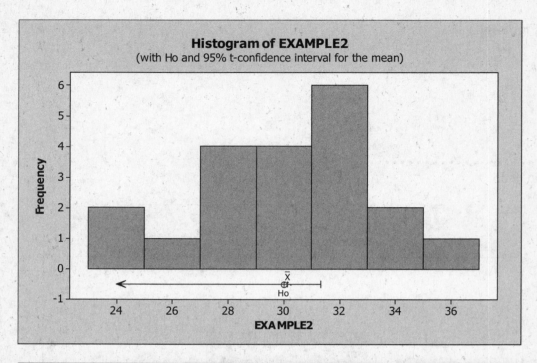

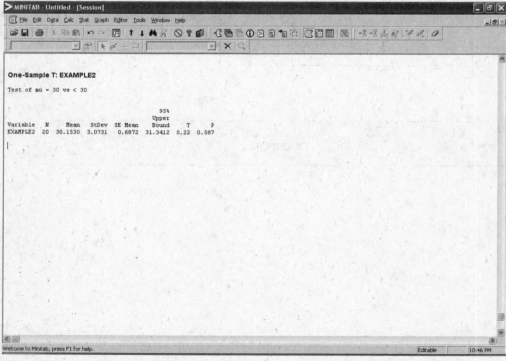

The graphs show the shape of the dataset: slightly skewed with no outliers. In the Session Window, notice that the p-value is P = .587. Since .587 is larger than our α = .01, we do NOT reject the null hypothesis. Thus, the owner's theory that couples spend, on average, less than $30 is not supported.

Tests for a Proportion

Hypothesis testing for a proportion is very simple. MINITAB can analyze raw data or summarized data. Raw data is usually in the form of YES or NO, representing the individual responses to a question with 2 possible answers. Summarized data *summarizes* the raw data and records the proportion of each answer in the sample.

Example 3:

For a practice example using raw data, we will use Example3 (C3) to do a hypothesis test. C3 contains data on a sample of 100 graduating seniors at a university who were asked: "Have you been offered a job in your field of study?" An employment counselor at the university believes that fewer than 60% of all graduating seniors end up with jobs in their fields of study. Test his belief using a hypothesis test for a proportion: H_0: p = .60 vs. H_A: p < .60 at α = .05.

Click on: STAT $\rightarrow$ BASIC STATISTICS $\rightarrow$ 1 PROPORTION

On the input screen that appears (Fig. 9-7), enter the following:

Samples in columns: Example 3

Fig. 9-7

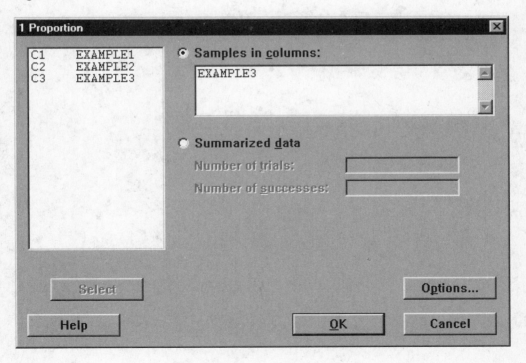

Next click on **Options** to select the null and alternative hypotheses and level of significance. Since we are testing if the population proportion is less than .60, enter:

> **Test proportion:** .60
> **Alternative:** less than

Click to select **Use test and interval based on normal distribution.**
(Fig. 9-8)

Fig. 9-8

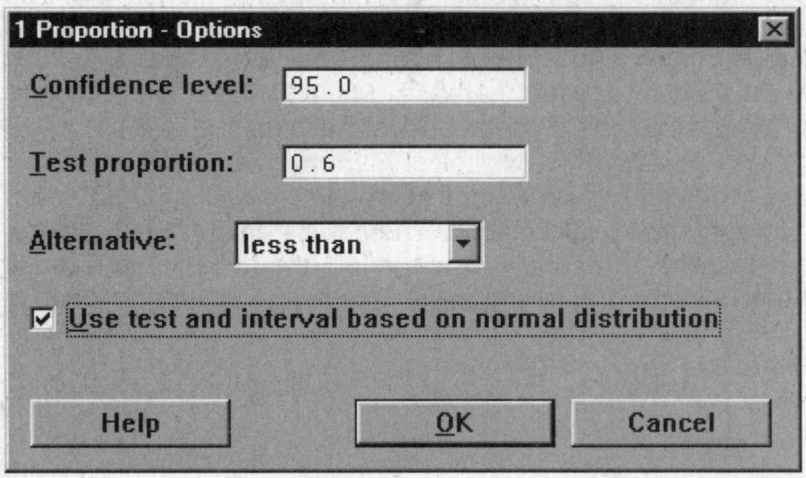

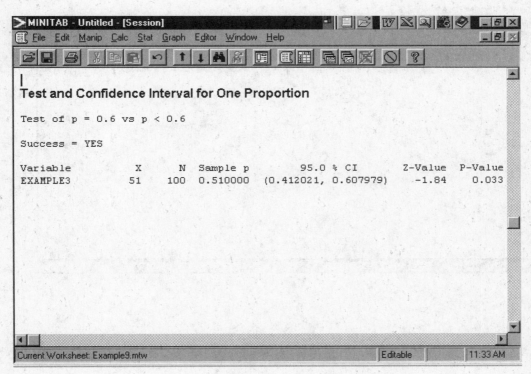

Click on **OK** twice, and the results should be in your Session Window (Fig. 9-9)

Fig. 9-9

The results show that P=.033, so we would REJECT the null hypothesis since .033 < .05, our α-level for this test. Thus we conclude that the nutritionist's belief is supported. (Fewer than 60% of these students are overweight.)

Example 4:

To run a hypothesis test about a proportion using summarized data, suppose we take a sample of 100 graduating seniors. We wish to check the published statistic that 40% complete their education in 4 years. It is found that only 28 in our sample actually finished in 4 years. At α = .05, test if the proportion is actually lower than 40%. Using the 1 Proportion test described above, STAT $\rightarrow$ BASIC STATISTICS $\rightarrow$ 1 PROPORTION, select **Summarized data** and enter the **Number of trials** (100) and the **Number of successes** (28). Then select **Options** and fill in the appropriate information. The results appear below in Fig. 9-9. Notice that the p-value is .007, and thus we reject the null hypothesis and conclude that fewer than 40% of graduating seniors completed their education in 4 years.

• •

Fig. 9-10

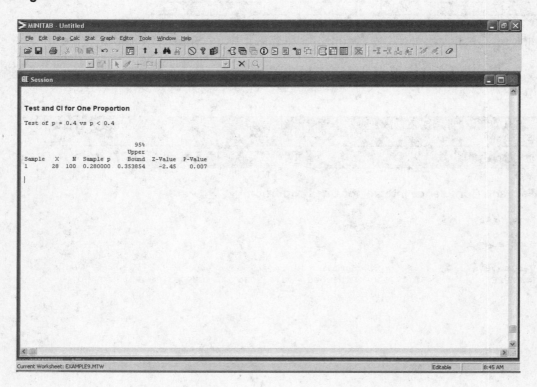

Assignment

• •

Please answer all questions in the space provided. When you have completed this assignment, tear the pages along the perforation. Include with this assignment all computer work that is required to answer the questions. Each graph must be labeled with a title, axis labels, and a footnote with your name and section number. If the assignment requires you to print the Session Window, click in the Session Window and type your name and section number so you can identify your printout.

1. A local university boasts that its School of Engineering attracts the top students from around the country. As proof of this claim, they say that the average Math SAT score for their students is higher than the average Math SAT score of 610 at most other Engineering schools. A random sample of n = 28 Engineering students is taken, and their Math SAT scores are recorded in MATHSAT1.MTW.

    a. What are the appropriate null and alternative hypotheses?

    b. Do a probability plot to look for normality. Report your findings here.

    c. What is the appropriate test of hypothesis to perform, a Z-test or a T-test? Why?

    d. Perform the test of hypothesis and include a Boxplot and a Histogram.

        What is the value of the test statistic? _____

        What is the P-value of the test? _____

        What is your decision using $\alpha = .01$? _____

        Are there any outliers? _____

        Is the data fairly symmetric? _____

Can this School brag that their students really are top-notch? Why or why not?

f. Estimate the average Math SAT score of this school's engineering students using a 95% confidence interval. Interpret the confidence interval.

2. Calcium is the most abundant and one of the most important minerals in the body. It works with phosphorus to build and maintain bones and teeth. According to the Food and Nutrition Board of the National Academy of Sciences, the recommended daily allowance (RDA) of calcium for adults is 800 milligrams. The data, saved as CALCIUM1.MTW, is the daily calcium intake (in mg.) for a sample of people with poverty level incomes. The researchers believe that the mean daily calcium intake for poverty level income people is below the recommended 800 mg. (poor people don't get enough milk, etc.). Assume that, from previous studies, $\sigma = 3.0$

a. What is the appropriate null and alternative hypotheses?

b. What is the appropriate test of hypothesis, a Z-test or a t-test? Why?

c. Do a boxplot and a histogram as part of the hypothesis test. Are there any outliers? Is the data symmetric?

d. What is the value of the test statistic? _____

What is the P-value of the test? _____

What is your decision, for $\alpha = .05$? _____

What is your conclusion about the calcium level of poor people?

3. The TV show *CSI* enjoyed tremendous popularity recently. During last year's season, it was claimed that 45% of college students name *CSI* as their favorite show. Fans of *West Wing* believed that percentage was inflated, so they decided to take a survey of 100 college students. Each student was asked the question: "Is *CSI* your favorite TV show?" Each person could answer either Yes or No. The data is found in TV1.MTW.

    a. State the appropriate null and alternative hypotheses.

    b. Perform the test of hypothesis.

        What is the test statistic? _____

        At $\alpha = .05$, what is your decision? _____

        Why?

        Write a short statement summarizing your results.

4. The national percentage of automobile accident fatalities which are alcohol related is 41%. In a random sample of 92 automobile accident fatalities in the

state of Connecticut, 45 were alcohol related. Is this sufficient evidence to say that Connecticut has a higher percentage of alcohol related automobile fatalities?

a. What are the appropriate null and alternative hypotheses?

b. Perform the test of hypothesis.

   What is the test statistic? _____

   What is the P-value of the test? _____

   At $\alpha = .05$, what is your decision? Why?

   Write a short statement summarizing your results.

Chapter 10

Comparing Two Populations

I N THIS CHAPTER, we will be making comparisons between two populations. Specifically, we will be looking at differences between population means.

The first step in our analysis is to determine the appropriate test procedure: "the 2-sample test" or the "matched pairs test." For the 2-sample test, the sampling is done by selecting a random sample from each of distinct two populations. For example, population 1 might be the Math Achievement scores for all students in the School of Business, and population 2, the Math Achievement scores for all students in the School of Education. Since these are two different schools, samples from these populations will be **independent**. For the matched pairs test, there will be some sort of relationship or "pairing" between observations from each sample. For example, population 1 could consist of scores on a Math Achievement test for all incoming freshmen and population 2 could consist of scores on the Achievement Test for these same students after they had taken one math course. Since both sets of scores are from the same students, the two populations are **dependent** and the observations in the samples are "paired."

**Note: All examples below use EXAMPLE10.MTW to demonstrate how to fill in the input screens.

Paired Difference Test

• •

When the data consists of two dependent samples (matched pairs), we are interested in the *differences* between the pairs of data points. In EXAMPLE10.MTW, C1 and C2 contain scores on Exam1 and Exam2 for a sample of 15 students who participated in a special tutorial session after taking Exam1. We are interested in seeing if their scores are higher on Exam 2 after taking the tutorial session.

To analyze this paired data in C1 and C2 of the file EXAMPLE10.MTW, we will use the "paired-t test." This test can be used for this small dataset (n=15) provided the data is approximately normal and does not contain any outliers.

Click on: STAT → BASIC STATISTICS → PAIRED t

This screen allows us to enter the actual data or the sample statistics (Fig. 10-1). Since we have the actual data in Columns 1 and 2, fill in the following:

    First Sample: C1
    Second Sample: C2

• •
Fig. 10-1

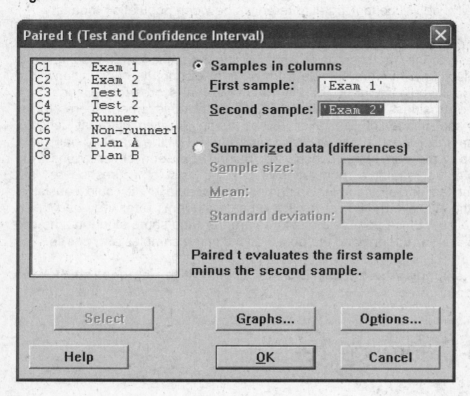

To check that the data is approximately normal and contains no outliers, click on **Graphs** and select **Histogram** and **Boxplot**.

The next step is to choose the appropriate alternative hypothesis. In the paired t-test, the null hypothesis is: H_0: $\mu_d = 0$. This simply states that the average difference between Exam1 and Exam2 scores is 0. In this example, we are testing to see if there is an improvement in test scores after the tutorial session. If there is an improvement, then Exam 2 scores should be higher than Exam1 scores. So, when the differences are calculated in Minitab: "first sample—second sample," the differences should be negative. Therefore, the alternative hypothesis should be H_A: $\mu_d < 0$. Let's use a significance level of .05.

Click on **Options**. In the box for **Test mean**, enter 0.0, for the null hypothesis. For the **Alternative**, click on the down arrow beside **Alternative** and select **less than.** (Fig. 10-2)

....
Fig. 10-2

Paired t - Options   ☒

Confidence level: [95.0   ]

Test mean: [0.0   ]

Alternative: [less than   ▼]

[Help   ]   [O K   ]   [Cancel   ]

Click on **OK** twice, and the graphs and the results of the hypothesis test will be displayed. (Fig. 10-3)

....
Fig. 10-3

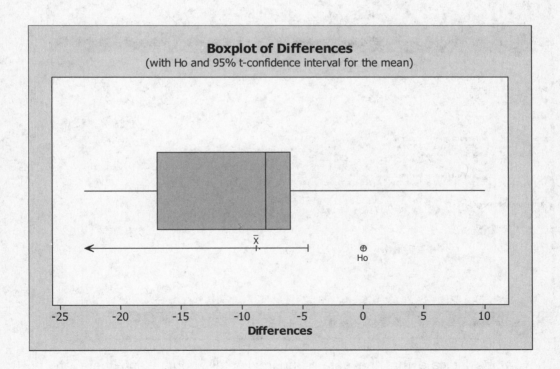

Boxplot of Differences
(with Ho and 95% t-confidence interval for the mean)

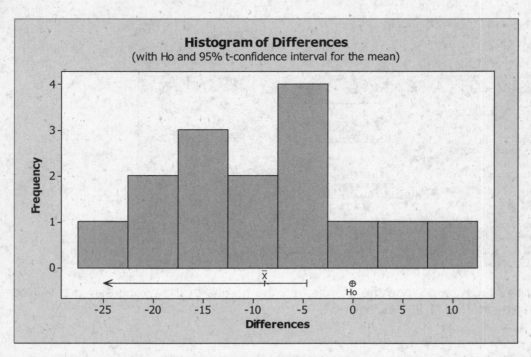

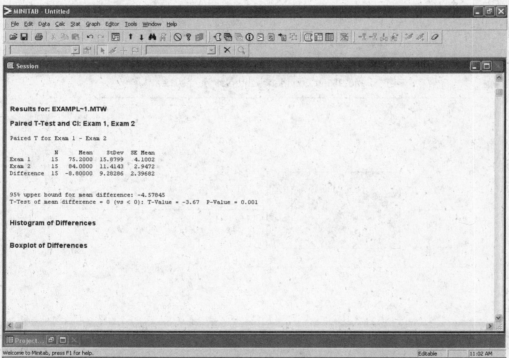

The graphs indicate that the data is approximately normal and there are no outliers. This justifies the use of the paired t-test.

Now, look at the Session Window. Notice that the P-value of the test is .001. This is significantly less than our α = .05, and so the special tutorial session appears to have been successful in raising the students' grades on Exam 2.

Note: If, from the Histogram and Boxplot, it is not clear that the data is approximately normal, you can do a Probability plot of the data. In order to do this plot, you first must create a column of differences.

Click on: Calc → Calculator

On the screen that appears, **store Result** in C3. For **Expression**, type in C1 – C2. Click on OK and C3 will now contain all the differences. Now create a probability plot of the data in C3 and evaluate it for normality.

Two Sample t-test:

· ·

When the data consists of two independent samples from normally distributed populations, the 2-sample t-test is the appropriate hypothesis test to use. In practice, the normality requirement is not absolutely essential. In large samples (n > 30), the test can be used even for non-normal distributions. Even in small samples (n < 30), the test can be used as long as the datasets are not extremely skewed and there are no extreme outliers.

When comparing two independent populations using a 2-sample t-test, we are interested in testing the difference between the means of the populations. The null hypothesis is that there is no difference between the two means ($\mu_1 = \mu_2$), and the alternative hypothesis is that there is a difference, ($\mu_1 \neq \mu_2$), ($\mu_1 > \mu_2$) or ($\mu_1 < \mu_2$).

Example 1:

Suppose we are interested in comparing the resting pulse rates of female marathon runners with those of female non-runners. We have a random sample of 20 runners in C5 and a random sample of 25 non-runners in C6 of the file EXAMPLE10.MTW.

Click on: GRAPH → PROBABILITY PLOTS and select Multiple. On the screen that appears, select C5 and C6 as your **Graph Variables.** Click on **OK**, and Normal Probability Plots of the data will appear. Recall that if the data points are fairly linear, then the data is approximately normal. P-values are printed at the right of the graph. If each p-value is greater than .05, assume normality for each dataset. (In this example, you will find that both samples are approximately normal.) (Fig. 10-4)

•••••••••••••••••••••
Fig. 10-4

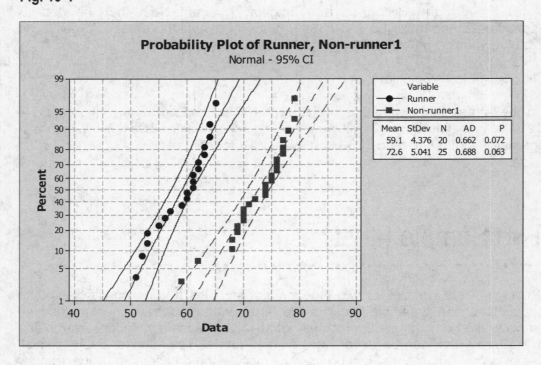

Now we are ready to proceed with the hypothesis test comparing the average pulse rates of the two groups. Specifically, we are interested in testing to see if female runners have an average pulse rate that is less than that of female non-runners. The appropriate test is H_o: $\mu_1 = \mu_2$ vs. H_a: $\mu_1 < \mu_2$. We will use a significance level of .05.

Click on: STAT → BASIC STATISTICS → 2-SAMPLE T and fill in the following fields: (Fig. 10-5)

Click on: **Samples in different Columns**:
                   First: C5
                   Second: C6

• •

Fig. 10-5

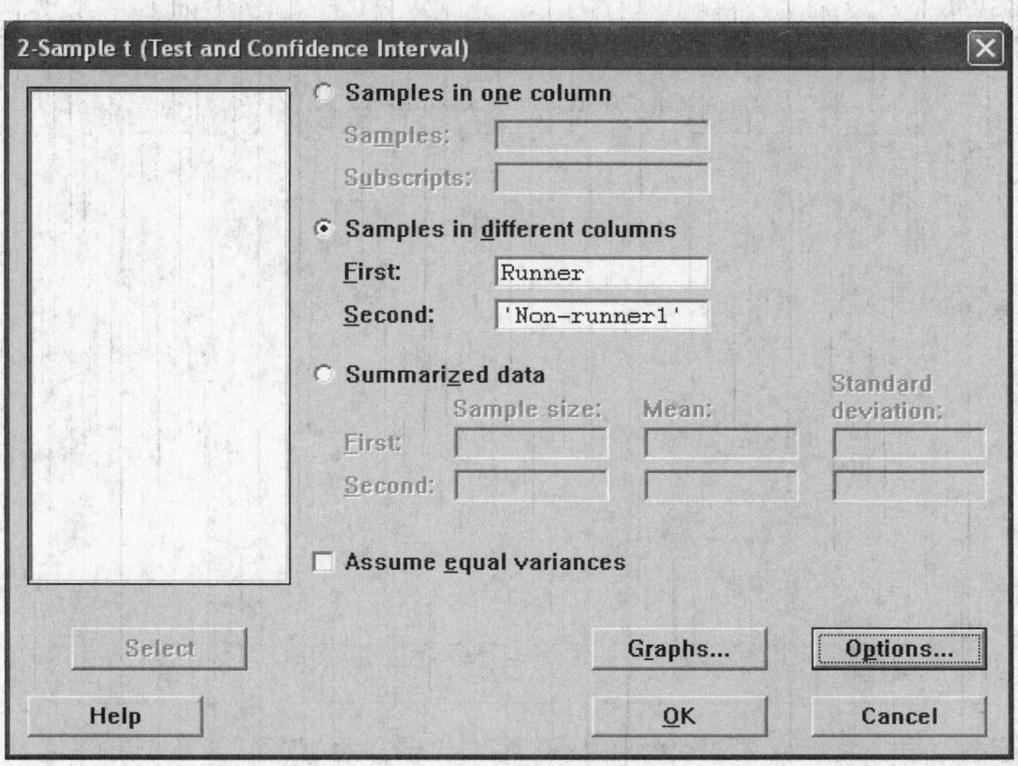

Click on: **Graphs** and select the Boxplot.

Click on: **Options**
                Test diff: 0.0
                Alternative: less than

Click on **OK** twice, and the Boxplots and the hypothesis test will be displayed. (Fig. 10-6)

Fig. 10-6

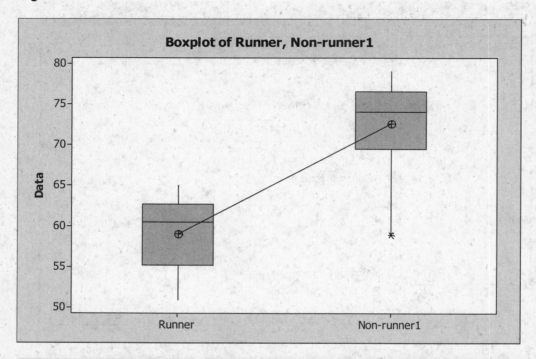

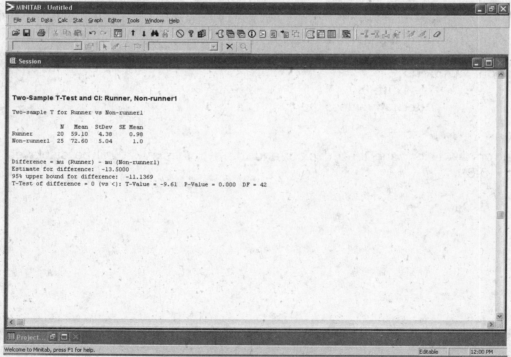

The Boxplots show one slight outlier for the Non-runners. Another interesting feature of the graph is the line connecting the means of the two groups. It certainly appears that there is a significant difference between the two means.

In the Session Window, you should see the test results and several additional pieces of information about each sample. The mean, standard deviation, and sample size are shown for each sample. Next look at the test statistic, T = -9.61, and the p-value, P=0.0000. Since P < .05, we would reject the null hypothesis, and conclude that there is overwhelming evidence that the average pulse rate for Runners is lower than the average pulse rate for Non-runners.

Example 2:

Suppose we are interested in comparing the test scores from the first two exams in an Introductory Statistics course of 500 students. A random sample of 100 test scores is selected from Test 1, and then another independent random sample of 100 scores from Test 2 is selected. Test 1 data is found in C3 and Test 2 data is in C4 of EXAMPLE10.MTW. Specifically, we are interested in determining whether there is a difference in the 2 population means. Note: this is not a "paired t-test" because the samples were selected independently from each of the two tests. So the appropriate test is H_o: $\mu_1 = \mu_2$ vs. H_a: $\mu_1 \neq \mu_2$. Suppose we use a significance level of .05.

Just click on: STAT $\rightarrow$ BASIC STATISTICS $\rightarrow$ 2-SAMPLE t.

Fill in the fields as follows:

Click on: **Samples in different Columns**:
                      First: C3
                      Second: C4

Click on: **Graphs** and select **Boxplots**

Click on: Click on: **Options**
                      Test diff: 0.0
                      Alternative: not equal

Click on **OK** twice, and the graph and hypothesis test should appear. (Fig. 10-7).

Fig. 10-7

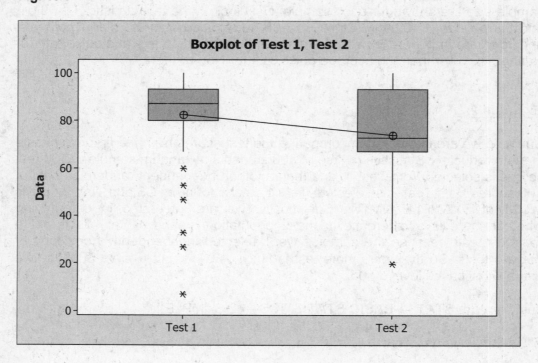

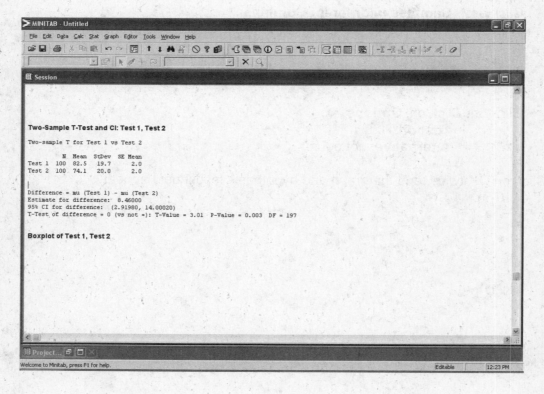

Several outliers appear in the Boxplots. Your next step should be to confirm that these are valid data points. Let's assume, for this example, all data points are valid data points. Because the samples are large, these outliers and the skewness in the datasets are not a concern.

Now look at the Session Window. The screen gives several pieces of information about each sample. The mean, standard deviation, and sample size are shown for each sample. Notice that the 95% confidence interval for $\mu_1 - \mu_2$ is (2.9, 14.0). This means that the average score on Test 1 was between 2.9 and 14 points higher than the average score on Test 2. Next look at the test statistic, T=3.01, and p-value, P=.003. Since P < .05 (our α-level), we would reject the null hypothesis ($\mu_1 = \mu_2$) and conclude that the average score on Test 1 was significantly higher than the average score on Test 2.

Note: The following section is an Optional Section dealing with Non-parametric tests.

Wilcoxon Rank-Sum Test
(also called the Mann-Whitney Test)
• •

In the previous section, we used the 2-sample t-test to test the difference in means from two independent populations. In the small sample case (n_1 or $n_2 <$ 30), a necessary condition was that the two populations were not extremely skewed and no outliers were present. If the data appears to be skewed or if there are outliers, the 2-sample t-test should not be used.

The Wilcoxon Rank-Sum test is another procedure for comparing two populations when using independent samples. This is called a **nonparametric** test and is used when the samples are small, the data is skewed and/or there are outliers. This test only requires that the two populations have approximately the same shape—but the shape can be anything—it can even be extremely skewed. The shape of the two samples can be compared using a stemplot. Unfortunately, even with a plot of the data, it is difficult to compare shapes with very small samples. So, unless the shapes are very different (i.e. one data set is skewed to the right and the other data set is skewed to the left), the Wilcoxon Rank-Sum test can be used.

In the Wilcoxon Rank-Sum test the null and alternative hypotheses are tests of medians rather than means. The median is used because it is a better measure of the center of the data when the data is not symmetric.

This test is especially simple to do using MINITAB. However, it is called the Mann-Whitney test in MINITAB. This is because two statisticians (Mann and Whitney) did some work on the test after Wilcoxon, so their names are sometimes used for the test.

As an example, we will look at Diet Plan A and Diet Plan B and try to determine which plan is more effective. We will use a significance level of .05. Suppose we have weight loss data from 15 subjects who followed Diet Plan A for one year in C7, and 13 subjects who followed Plan B for one year in C8. Since the samples are small, we must address the question of shape and the question of outliers. A stemplot can accomplish this for us. (Fig. 10-8)

• •

Fig. 10-8

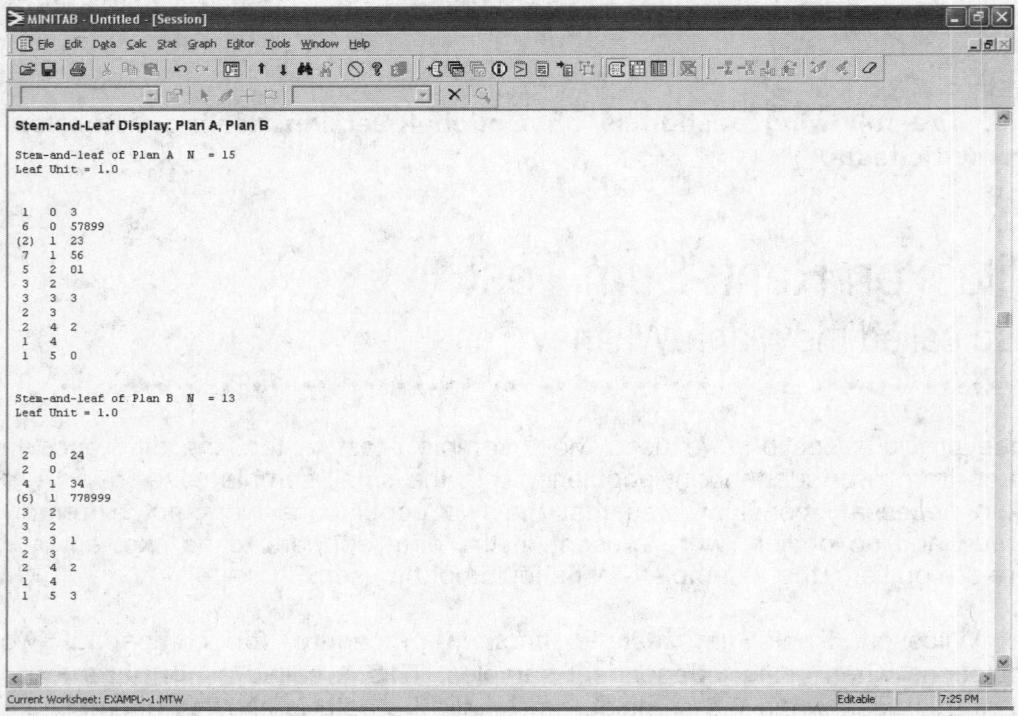

As you can see from the plots, both datasets are skewed to the right. So we will proceed with the non-parametric test of hypothesis.

Click on: STAT → NONPARAMETRICS → MANN-WHITNEY

On the input screen, fill in the two columns where the data is stored, and select the proper alternative hypothesis. (Fig. 10-9)

• •

Fig. 10-9

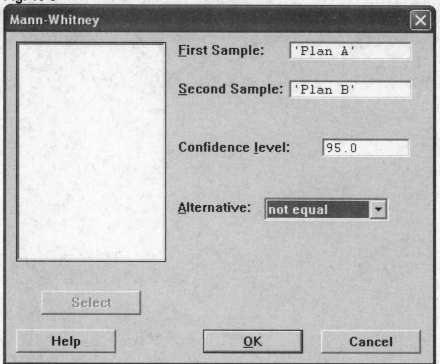

Then click on **OK**, and the results of the test should appear in the Session Window. (Fig. 10-10)

• •
Fig. 10-10

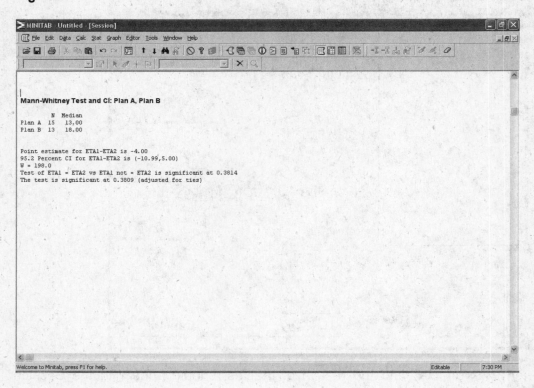

In the MINITAB output, notice that the Wilcoxon Rank-Sum Test compares the medians of the two samples instead of the means. The population medians are called ETA1 and ETA2. Also notice in Fig. 10-10 that the above test "is significant at 0.3814". This is the P-value. The next line on the output is another P-value, 0.3809, which MINITAB calculates when there are ties in the data. These P-values will always be very close. The adjusted P-value is the correct one to use when it appears in the output. Since .3809 is greater than .05, our α-level, we would fail to reject the null hypothesis. Thus, there is no significant difference in the two diet plans.

Assignment

• •

Please answer all questions in the space provided. When you have completed this assignment, tear the pages along the perforation. Include with this assignment all computer work that is required to answer the questions. Each graph must be labeled with a title, axis labels, and a footnote with your name and section number. If the assignment requires you to print the Session Window, click in the Session Window and type your name and section number so you can identify your printout.

1. Compare the Math SAT scores of students in the School of Engineering with students in the School of Business. Suppose you suspect that the engineering students will have a higher average SAT score, and you would like to do a test of hypothesis to check if your suspicions are confirmed. The data is stored in MATHSAT1.MTW.

    a. Are the populations independent or dependent? Explain.

    b. Do probability plots of the datasets and report your results below. Specifically, for each data is the data linear? What is the p-value? What does the p-value tell you about the normality of each dataset?

    School of Engineering:

    School of Business:

    c. What is the appropriate test to perform? Is it a paired-t test or a two sample t-test? Why?

    d. What are the appropriate null and alternative hypotheses for the test?

e. Using $\alpha = .05$, perform the appropriate test of hypothesis in MINITAB. What are the results of the test?

f. What conclusion can you make about the Math SAT scores of students in the engineering and business schools?

2. Students applying to law school must take the LSAT exam. Since competition for acceptance is stiff, many students take a course which is advertised to boost scores on the LSAT. The agency that teaches the course claims the course is an effective way to raise scores on the LSAT. To test this claim, a group of students are given the LSAT and their scores are recorded. They then attend the course for 5 weeks and retake the exam. Their scores are recorded again. The test scores are saved in LSAT1.MTW

a. Are the populations independent or dependent? Explain.

b. What is the appropriate test of hypothesis to perform? Is it the paired t-test or the 2-sample t-test? Why?

c. Using $\alpha = .05$, perform the appropriate test of hypothesis in MINITAB. Include a Histogram and a Boxplot of the data.

      d. Summarize the data based on the graphs. Specifically, address skewness and outliers.

      e. What are the results of the test?

      f. What conclusion can you make about the effectiveness of the LSAT preparation course?

      g. Use the 95% confidence interval to estimate the average difference between the pre-scores and post-scores. Write a statement about the average difference using the confidence interval.

3. A professor teaches two large lecture classes in Psychology. In Class 1, students are required to participate in weekly study groups. In Class 2, there are no such requirements. The professor would like to see if the average

grade is higher for students who attend the study sessions. The data is stored in FINAL1.MTW.

a. Are the populations independent or dependent? Explain.

b. Using α = .05, perform the appropriate test of hypothesis in MINITAB. Include a Histogram and a Boxplot of the data.

c. Summarize the data based on the graphs. Specifically, address skewness and outliers.

d. What are the results of the test?

e. What conclusion can you make about the effectiveness of the weekly study sessions?

Optional Question on non-parametrics:

4. Suppose you would like to compare the average salary of American League baseball players to the average salary of National League players. Is there any difference between the average salary for the two teams? The data from two randomly selected teams is stored in BASEBALL1.MTW. C1 is an AL team and C2 is a NL team.

   a. Is it appropriate to assume normality here? Why or why not?

   b. Do a stemplot of the data so that you can compare the shape of the two samples. Describe the shapes of the two samples.

   c. What is the appropriate test of hypothesis? Why?

   d. Write the null and alternative hypotheses.

   e. Perform the test of hypothesis using $\alpha = .05$. Interpret the results using the p-value.

   f. What can you conclude about the average salaries of players on these two teams?

Chapter 11

Regression Analysis

N THIS CHAPTER on Regression Analysis, we consider relationships between two variables. For example, we might collect data on the number of hours individuals spend exercising per month and the weight loss for each individual. Or, we might be interested in the average number of hours 4th graders spend reading each week and their scores on a standardized reading test at the end of 4th grade. Or, we might be interested in the Verbal SAT score and the Math SAT score for incoming freshmen at a local university.

The first question we will ask is: "Are the two variables **related**?" For example, "Do students' scores on the Math SAT and Verbal SAT follow a pattern? Do students who score higher on the Math SAT test also tend to have higher scores on the Verbal SAT? Do students who score lower on the Math SAT test tend to score lower on the Verbal SAT?"

The second question, we might ask is: "Can one of the variables be used to **predict** the other variable?" Can we predict an individual's weight loss based on the hours spent exercising per month? Or, can we predict a student's score on a reading test based on the number of hours spent reading?"

**Note: All examples below use EXAMPLE11.MTW to demonstrate how to fill in the input screens.

Scatterplots

••

The first step in our analysis is to graph the data using a scatterplot. In a scatterplot, one of the variables is labeled the "x-variable" and the other one the "y-variable." If your goal is to simply see how the variables are related (as with the Math and Verbal SAT scores) it doesn't matter which one you label as the x-variable and which one as the y-variable. If your goal is to use one of the variables to predict the other one, then the **predictor** must be the x-variable, and the y-variable is called the **response** variable.

Example 1: We will look at a small sample of data from 4th grade students. The two variables are "average hours spent reading per week" and "score on a reading test at the end of 4th grade." In this example, we would like to be able to **predict** the "reading test score" based on "the average hours spent reading per week." So, the x-variable (predictor) is "average hours spent reading per week" and the y-variable (response) is "reading test score."

Open the file labeled Example11.MTW. The first two columns contain the 4th grade information.

To construct a Scatterplot, click on **Graph→Scatterplot.** On the Input screen that appears, select the **Simple scatterplot.** Click on **OK.** (Fig. 11-1)

• •

Fig. 11-1

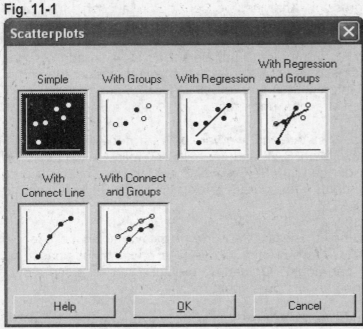

On the next input screen, enter C2 for the **Y-variables** and C1 for the **X-variables.** (Fig. 11-2)

• •

Fig. 11-2

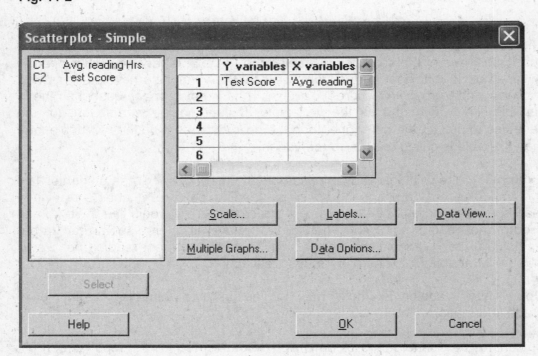

Click on **OK** and a scatter diagram of the data will be displayed. (Fig. 11-3)

• •

Fig. 11-3

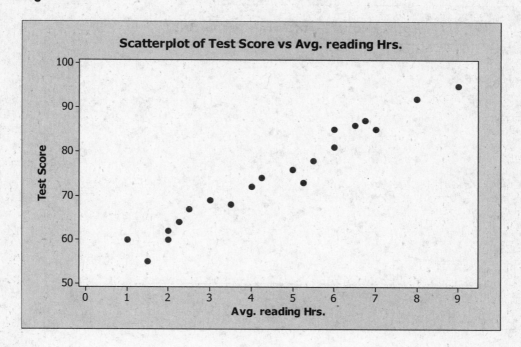

As you can see from the scatterplot, there appears to be a strong linear trend. The trend is positive because as the "average hours spent reading per week" increase, the "reading test score" also increases.

Example 2: For this example, we will look at a set of Math and Verbal SAT scores. We would like to see what type of relationship exists between the two variables. We are not interested in using one of the variables to predict the other variable so it does not matter which one is labeled as the x-variable and which one is the y-variable.

The data is contained in C3 and C4 of the Example11.MTW file.

To construct a Scatterplot, click on **Graph→Scatterplot.** Select the **Simple scatterplot.**

On the next input screen, enter C3 for the **Y-variables** and C4 for the **X-variables.** Click on **OK** and a scatter diagram of the data will be displayed. (Fig. 11-4).

Fig. 11-4

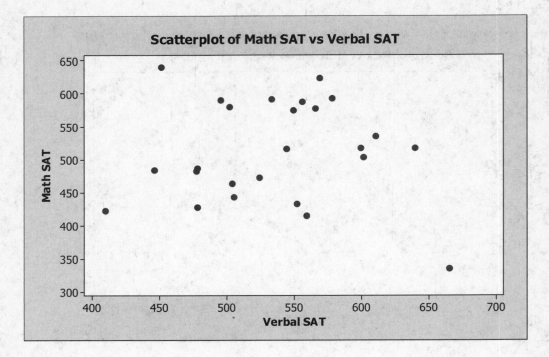

This plot looks like a scatter of points. There does not appear to be a relationship between Math SAT scores and Verbal SAT scores.

The purpose of the scatterplot is to determine what type of relationship exists between the two variables. In these two examples, you saw one relationship that appeared to follow a linear trend and another one that simply looked like a scatter. Of course, the graphs may show other types of patterns: quadratic, exponential or logarithmic, for example.

Correlation

If the scatterplot that is created for a set of data shows a linear trend, the next step is to measure the strength of the linear relationship between the two variables. The measurement that we use is called a "correlation coefficient." There are several different formulas for correlation coefficients. The most frequently used one is the "Pearson product moment correlation coefficient." It is labeled with the variable, r, and the formula is

$$r = \frac{\sum(x - \bar{x})(y - \bar{y})}{\sqrt{(x - \bar{x})^2(y - \bar{y})^2}}$$

Possible values for r range from -1 to +1. If the dataset has an r = +1, then the data points would all fall exactly on a line with a positive slope. If the dataset has an r = -1, then the data points would all fall exactly on a line with a negative slope. Datasets that have no linear pattern would have r-values equal to 0 or very close to 0. So, the r-value is a measure of how closely the data fits around a line drawn through the dataset.

Example 3: Calculate the correlation coefficient for the 4th grade reading data.

Click on **Stat → Basic Statistics → Correlation.** On the input screen, enter C1 and C2 for **Variables**.

Click on **OK.** The value of r, the correlation coefficient, will be displayed in the Session Window. (Fig. 11-5)

• •

Fig. 11-5

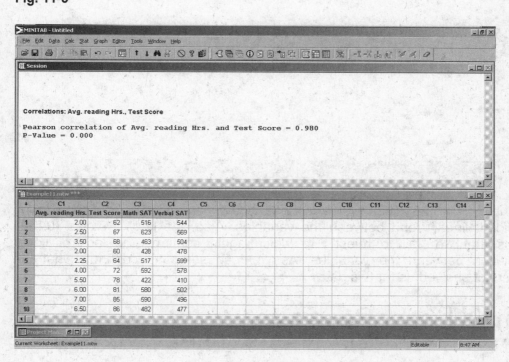

In this example, r = 0.98. This indicates a strong linear relationship between the "average hours spent reading per week" and "reading test score." Notice the P-value = 0.000. This P-value is the result of the hypothesis test: H$_o$:"There is **no linear correlation** between the variables" and H$_a$: "There **is a linear correlation** between the variables." Since the P-value is 0.000, we reject H$_o$ in favor of H$_a$ and conclude that there is a linear correlation between the variables. This is exactly what we expected because the scatterplot showed a very strong linear trend.

Example 4: Calculate the correlation coefficient for the Math and Verbal SAT scores. Click on **Stat → Basic Statistics → Correlation.** On the input screen, enter C3 and C4 for **Variables**. Click on **OK.** The value of r, the correlation coefficient, will be displayed in the Session Window. (Fig. 11-6)

• •

Fig. 11-6

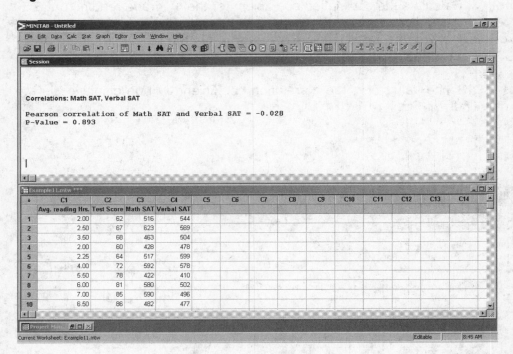

This time r = -0.28. This r-value is close to 0 which indicates that there is no significant linear trend between the variables. Also, the large P-value (0.893) means that we "fail to reject" H_o, which again confirms the lack of linear correlation between the variables. As you can see, this confirms what the scatterplot showed us for this data.

Simple Linear Regression:
• •

Now that we have looked at a graph of the data, our next question is to see if there is a simple mathematical function that can be fit through the data. The simplest function that can be used is a "linear function" which we write as y = a + bx, where "a" is the y-intercept and "b" is the slope. A linear function is appropriate when the data appears to fall along a straight line. Of course, the data will not follow exactly along a straight line. So our goal is to try to find the best fitting line for the data. The actual method for finding the best fitting line, called "the Regression line," involves the use of Calculus and a method called "minimizing the squared deviations from the line."

Example 3: Let's go back to the data in Example 1. The two variables, stored in C1 and C2 of the worksheet are "average hours spent reading per week" and "score on a reading test at the end of 4th grade." We already saw from the scatterplot and from the correlation that the data follows a linear pattern. What we would like to do now is to find the best fitting line for the data. We can then use this linear equation to **predict** the "reading test score" based on "the average hours spent reading per week." So, the x-variable, "average hours spent reading per week," is the **Predictor** and the y-variable, "reading test score," is the **Response**.

To find the regression equation, click on **Stat → Regression → Regression**. Enter C2 for the **Response** variable, and C1 as the **Predictor**. (Fig. 11-7)

• •

Fig. 11-7

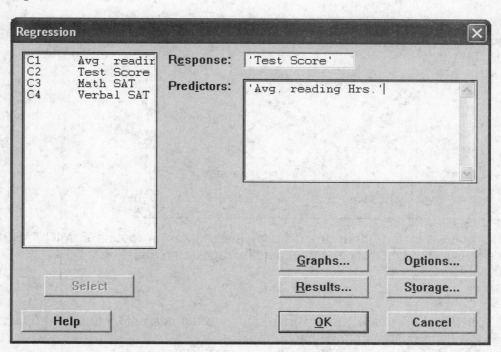

Click on **OK** and the results will be displayed in the Session Window. (Fig. 11-8)

• •

Fig. 11-8

Regression Analysis: Test Score versus Avg. reading Hrs.

```
The regression equation is
Test Score = 52.2 + 4.89 Avg. reading Hrs.


Predictor   Coef SE Coef T  P
Constant    52.207 1.171 44.57 0.000
Avg. reading Hrs. 4.8885 0.2310 21.17 0.000


S = 2.31482 R-Sq = 96.1% R-Sq(adj) = 95.9%


Analysis of Variance

Source   DF  SS   MS   F   P
Regression  1 2400.5 2400.5 447.99 0.000
Residual Error 18 96.5  5.4
Total   19 2496.9


Unusual Observations

  Avg.
  reading
Obs  Hrs. Test Score  Fit SE Fit Residual St Resid
 14  1.50  55.000 59.540 0.874 -4.540  -2.12R
 17  5.25  73.000 77.872 0.542 -4.872  -2.16R

R denotes an observation with a large standardized residual.
```

There is quite a lot of output produced by the regression routine in MINITAB. Let's begin with the first item of the output: the regression equation.

Test Score = 52.2 + 4.89 Avg. reading Hrs.

In this equation, 52.2 is the y-intercept, rounded to the nearest tenth, and 4.89 is the slope, rounded to the nearest hundredth.

The equation shows us how to "predict" a student's test score based on the average number of hours spent reading per week. For example, if a student spent an average of 8.5 hours reading per week, then we would predict his/her test score to be: 52.2 + 4.89 * 8.5 = 93.765.

In the section below the equation, under the heading "Coef" (coefficient), you see the y-intercept (52.207) and the slope (4.8885). The slope is an important statistic because it is a measure of the relationship between x and y. Specifically, the slope is the "change in y divided by the change in x." To understand the slope it is easier to think of it as a fraction. So, 4.8885 can be written as 4.8885 divided by 1. This tells us that for every 1 unit change in x, y changes by 4.8885 units. In terms of our example, for every additional one hour of reading, the test score will increase by 4.8885 points.

In the next section, the standard error, s, is displayed. This is an indication of the variation or scatter, around the line. Small "s" values indicate less scatter around the line; large "s" values indicate more scatter around the line.

The next item is the R-sq value of 96.1%. This R-sq value, which is also called the coefficient of determination, measures the amount of variation in the y-values that is explained by the x-values. The closer this value is to 100%, the better the regression model is at describing the data.

The final section is a list of "Unusual Observations." This is a list of data points that have been calculated as points that differ significantly from the rest of the data. It is important to check these points and be certain that they are not erroneous data values.

We can actually get a picture of the scatterplot along with the fitted line. This way we can see how closely the points fit around the line. If the points are clustered tightly around the line the standard error will be small and the R-sq value will be large (close to 100%).

To plot the graph with the fitted line, click on **Stat → Regression → Fitted Line Plot.** Enter C2 for the **Response** variable, and C1 as the **Predictor.** For **Type of Regression Model** select **Linear**. Click on OK. (Fig. 11-9)

• •
Fig. 11-9

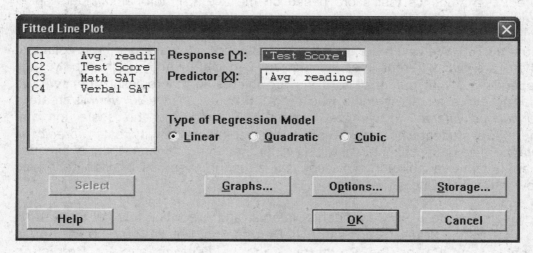

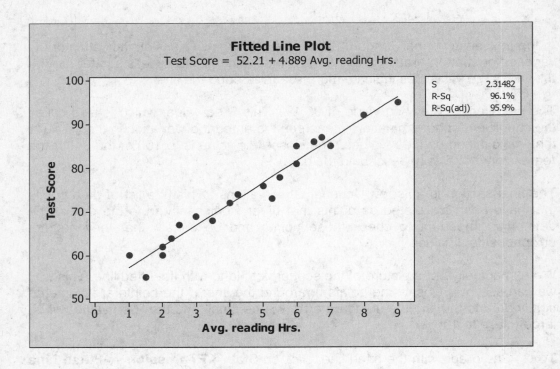

In addition to the above output, the regression calculation has an option that allows us to calculate "confidence intervals" and "prediction intervals" for specific x-values. Recall the regression equation that we calculated from the sample data: Test Score = 52.2 + 4.89 Avg. reading Hrs. The equation shows us how to "predict" a student's test score based on the average number of hours spent reading per week. For example, suppose a student spent an average of 8.5 hours reading per week. We would predict his/her test score to be: 52.2 + 4.89 * 8.5 = 93.765. We would like to create a confidence interval around this estimate. There are two different intervals that we can create and which one we use depends on what our goal is. If we are interested in predicting the **average** reading score for all students who read 8.5 hours per week, we will create a *confidence interval*. If we are interested in predicting the score for **one individual** student who read 8.5 hours per week then we will create a *prediction interval*. The prediction interval will be wider than the confidence interval because there is more variability in individual values than in averages. Minitab generates both intervals in one step.

To begin, create a 95% confidence interval and prediction interval for x = 8.5 hours. Click on **Stat → Regression → Regression.** Enter C2 for the **Response** variable, and C1 as the **Predictor.** Click on **Options** and for **Prediction intervals for new observations**, enter 8.5. Select both **Confidence limits** and **Prediction limits**. (Fig. 11-10)

Fig. 11-10

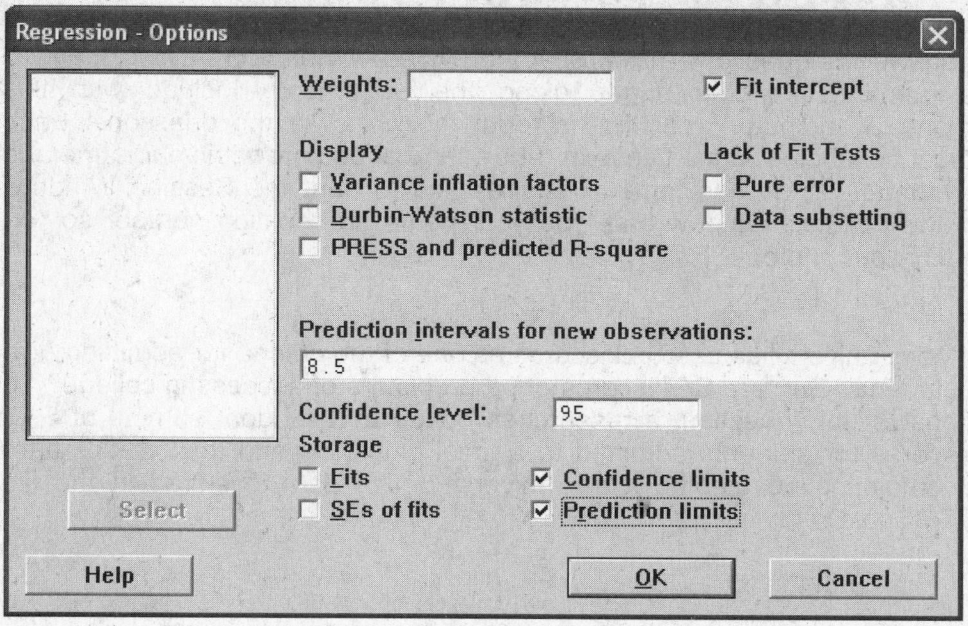

Click on **OK** twice and the regression results will appear in the Session Window. The following figure is the last section of the Regression output which displays the confidence intervals and predictions. (Fig. 11-11)

Fig. 11-11

```
Predicted Values for New Observations

New
Obs  Fit SE Fit  95% CI     95% PI
 1 93.760 1.049 (91.556, 95.963) (88.420, 99.099)


Values of Predictors for New Observations

  Avg.
New reading
Obs  Hrs.
 1  8.50
```

The output displays the predicted value, labeled "fit" for x =8.5. So someone who reads 8.5 hours is predicted to score 93.76 on the test. The next value in the row is a standard deviation that is used in calculating the confidence interval and the prediction interval. The 95% CI for the average score for all students who read 8.5 hours per week is (91.556, 95.963). The 95% prediction interval for an individual who read 8.5 hours per week is (88.420, 99.099). Notice that the prediction interval is wider than the confidence interval. Below this output is the value of the predictor, which is 8.5.

Assignment

• •

Please answer all questions in the space provided. When you have completed this assignment, tear the pages along the perforation. Include with this assignment all computer work that is required to answer the questions. Each graph must be labeled with a title, axis labels, and a footnote with your name and section number. If the assignment requires you to print the Session Window, click on the Session Window and type your name and section number so you can identify your printout.

1. Many universities use SAT scores as one of the criteria for admitting new students. But, are SAT scores good predictors of success in college? To answer this question, a researcher looked at a random sample of SAT scores for students admitted to a local university and their GPA's after completing 60 credits at the university. The data is stored in the file SatScor1.mtw.

   a. Plot the data.

   b. Describe the plot.

   c. Calculate and interpret the correlation coefficient, r.

   d. Create the regression line and write the equation here.

   e. What is the R-sq value? _____ What does it tell you about the regression?

f.   Create a 95% confidence interval for the average GPA for all students with an SAT score of 1300.

g.   Create a 95% prediction interval for the GPA for a student with an SAT score of 1300.

h.   Are there any unusual values? If so, what are they?

i.   Create a graph of the data with the fitted line plot. On the printout, circle the unusual values.

2.   The Math Department at a local community college has designed the math curriculum with a focus on problem solving. Consequently, they believe that scores on the reading placement test given to all entering students will be a good predictor of success in Math courses. To support their claim, they took a sample of students and recorded their reading placement test scores and their final exam scores from a problem solving math course. The data is stored in the file MathFinal1.mtw.

a.   Plot the data.

b.   Describe the plot.

c.   Calculate and interpret the correlation coefficient, r.

d.   Create the regression line and write the equation here.

e. What is the R-sq value? _____ What does it tell you about the regression?

f. Create a 95% confidence interval for the average final exam score for all students with a reading placement test score of 82.

g. Create a 95% prediction interval for the final exam score for a student with a reading placement test score of 82.

h. Are there any unusual values? If so, what are they?

i. Create a graph of the data with the fitted line plot. On the printout, circle the unusual values.